MᶜGUFFEY'S®

ECLECTIC

SPELLING-BOOK.

REVISED EDITION.

McGuffey Editions and Colophon are Trademarks of
VAN NOSTRAND REINHOLD
New York

PREFACE.

In revising this book, care has been taken to preserve all the excellences that have so long and so favorably distinguished McGuffey's Eclectic Spelling-Book: and the chief changes that have been made, have been suggested by the evident plan of the original work.

The old system of indicating the pronunciation by numerals, called "superiors," has been abandoned, and the diacritical marks used by Webster have been adopted. The Revised Speller conforms in orthography, pronunciation, and syllabication to the latest edition of Webster's Unabridged Dictionary. Exercises have been given on each of the distinctive marks used in the book, as will be seen by reference to Lessons 36–57.

A number of lessons have been added in the department of prefixes and suffixes, and now nearly all the more common of these etymological principles have been explained. (See Lessons 136–167.)

In arranging the text of the several lessons, the object has been not to appeal merely to arbitrary memory, but to associate each lesson with some principle of sound, meaning, or accent, which would tend to aid the pupil in acquiring a knowledge of our language. Several distinct lessons on pronunciation are given, and towards the close of the book numerous lessons of difficult words in orthography have been introduced.

Instead of indicating silent letters by italics, as has hitherto been done, a new type has been made in which such letters are canceled, thus enabling the pupil to discover their *status* at a glance.

The pages have been enlivened, as in the other books of this Series, by attractive engravings.

The publishers take pleasure in acknowledging the valuable services of W. B. Watkins, D. D., who planned and executed this revision.

DECEMBER, 1879.

THE ENGLISH ALPHABET.

The **English Alphabet** consists of twenty-six letters, viz.: *a, b, c, d, e, f, g, h, i, j, k, l, m, n, o, p, q, r, s, t, u, v, w, x, y, z.*

Letters are divided into Vowels and Consonants.

The **Vowels** are those letters which can be perfectly sounded without the aid of any other letter. The vowels are *a, e, i, o, u, w,* and *y.*

The vowel sounds of *w* and *y* are the same as those of *u* and *i.* *A, e,* and *o* are always vowels. *I, u, w,* and *y* are sometimes consonants.

A **Diphthong** is the union of two vowels in one sound.

When *both* vowels are sounded, the diphthong is called Proper, because then it is really a Diphthong, or *double sound;* that is, the sounds of the vowels unite; as, *oi* in *oil; ou* in *sound.*

When only *one* of the vowels is sounded, the diphthong is called Improper, because then, as one of the vowels is silent, it is not *properly* a Diphthong, though it takes that name; as, *oa* in *boat, ui* in *suit,* where *a* and *i* are silent.

The following diphthongs are in common use, viz.: *oi, oy, ou, ow, ae, ai, au, aw, ay, ea, ei, eo, eu, ew, ey, ia, ie, oa, oe, ua, ue, ui;* as in *toil, boy, round, plow, seal, coal, head, sail, say, aught, yeoman.* Of these, *oi, oy, ou,* and *ow* are generally proper diphthongs; though sometimes *ou* and *ow* are improper, as in *famous,* where *o* is silent, and in *slow,* where *w* is silent.

A **Triphthong** is the union of *three* vowels in one syllable; as, *eau* in *beau, iew* in *view.* The triphthong is properly a union of *letters,* not *sounds.*

OF THE VARIOUS SOUNDS.

All the vowels, and some of the consonants, have several sounds; in this book these sounds are indicated by *diacritical marks*, as in the following tables:

TABLE OF VOCALS.

Long Sounds.

ā,	as in āte.		ē,	as in ēve.
â,	" câre.		ẽ,	" ẽrr.
ä,	" ärm.		ī,	" īçe.
à,	" làst.		ō,	" ōde.
ạ,	" ạll.		ū,	" ūse.

ōō, as in fōōl.

Short Sounds.

ă,	as in ăm.		ŏ,	as in ŏdd.
ĕ,	" ĕlm.		ŭ,	" ŭp.
ĭ,	" ĭn.		ŏŏ,	" lŏŏk.

Diphthongs.

oi, oy, as in oil, boy.		ou, ow, as in out, owl.

TABLE OF SUBVOCALS.

b,	as in bĭb.		v,	as in vălve.
d,	" dĭd.		th,	" thĭs.
g̅,	" g̅ĭg̅.		z,	" zĭnc.
j,	" jŭg̅.		zh,	" äzure.
n,	" nīne.		r,	" râre.
m,	" māim.		w,	" wē.
ng,	" hăng.		y,	" yĕt.

l, as in lŭll.

TABLE OF ASPIRATES.

f,	as in fīfe.		t,	as in tärt.
h,	" hĭm.		sh,	" shē.
k,	" cāke.		ch,	" chăt.
p,	" pīpe.		th,	" thĭck.
s,	" sāme.		wh,	" whȳ.

NOTE.—The foregoing forty-four sounds are those most employed in the English language. Some of these sounds are represented by other letters, as shown in the following table. For further instruction concerning the sounds, see Lessons 36–57.

TABLE OF SUBSTITUTES.

ạ,	for	ŏ,	as in	whạt.	ў,	for	ĭ,	as in	mўth.
ê,	"	â,	"	thêre.	ȼ,	"	k,	"	ȼăn.
ẹ,	"	ā,	"	fẹint.	ç,	"	s,	"	çīte.
ï,	"	ē,	"	polïçe.	çh,	"	sh,	"	çhāiẹe.
ĩ,	"	ẽ,	"	sĩr.	ȼh,	"	k,	"	ȼhāos.
ó,	"	ŭ,	"	són.	ġ,	"	j,	"	ġĕm.
ọ,	"	ōō,	"	tọ.	ṉ,	"	ng,	"	ĭṉk.
ǫ,	"	ŏŏ,	"	wǫlf.	ẓ,	"	z,	"	ăẓ.
ô,	"	ạ,	"	fôrk.	ṣ,	"	sh,	"	suṛe.
õ,	"	ẽ,	"	wõrk.	x̱,	"	gz,	"	ĕx̱ăȼt.
u̧,	"	ŏŏ,	"	fu̧ll.	gh,	"	f,	"	läugh.
û,	"	ẽ,	"	bûrn.	ph,	"	f,	"	phlŏx.
u̶,	"	ōō,	"	ru̶de.	qu,	"	k,	"	pïque.*
ȳ,	"	ī,	"	flȳ.	qu,	"	kw,	"	quĭt.

W, in its vowel sounds, corresponds with ū; as in *new* (*pro*. nū). *A* has, in a few words, the sound of ĕ; as in *any* (*pro*. ĕn′nў). *U* has, in a few words, the sound of ĕ; as in *bury* (*pro*. bĕr′ry); or that of ĭ, as in *busy* (*pro*. bĭz′ў).

OF THE CONSONANTS.

The **Consonants** are those letters which can not be perfectly sounded without the aid of a vowel. The consonants are *b, c, d, f, g, h, j, k, l, m, n, p, q, r, s, t, v, x, z,* and sometimes *i, u, w,* and *y.* The consonants are divided into MUTES and SEMI-VOWELS.

The **Mutes** are those consonants that admit of no sound without the aid of a vowel. They are *b, d, k, p, q, t,* and *c* and *g* hard.

*NOTE.—The *u* is canceled in this book when *qu* is sounded like *k*.

The **Semi-vowels** are those consonants that can be sounded imperfectly by themselves. They are *f, h, j, l, m, n, r, s, v, x, z,* and *c* and *g* soft.

Four of the semi-vowels are called Liquids; viz., *l, m, n,* and *r.* They are called liquids because they unite so readily with other sounds, or flow into them.

OF SYLLABLES AND WORDS.

A **Syllable** is a sound, or a combination of sounds, uttered by a single impulse of the voice : it may have one or more letters; as, *a, bad, bad-ness.*

A **Word** is either a syllable or a combination of syllables; as, *not, notion.*

A word of one syllable is called a **Monosyllable**; as, *man.*

A word of two syllables is called a **Dissyllable**; as, *manly.*

A word of three syllables is called a **Trisyllable**; as, *manliness.* Words of more than three syllables are called **Polysyllables.**

Accent is a stress of voice placed upon some one syllable more than the others. Every word composed of two or more syllables has one of them accented. This accent is denoted by a mark (') at the end of the accented syllable; as, *mid'night, a ban'don.*

A **Primitive Word** is one which is not derived from any other word; as, *man, great, full.*

A **Derivative Word** is one which is formed from some other word by adding something to it; as, *manful, greatness, fully.*

A **Simple Word** is one which is not composed of more than one word; as, *kind, man, stand, ink.*

A **Compound Word** is one that is composed of two or more simple words; as, *ink-stand, wind-mill.*

Spelling is naming or writing the letters of a word.

Script Alphabet.

CAPITAL LETTERS.

A B C D E F G H I

J K L M N O P Q R

S T U V W X Y Z

LOWER-CASE LETTERS.

a b c d e f g h i

j k l m n o p q r

s t u v w x y z

THE ALPHABET.

A   B   C   D

E   F   G   H

I   J   K   L

M   N   O   P

Q   R   S   T

U   V   W   X

Y   Z

THE ALPHABET.

---

a	b	c	d
e	f	g	h
i	j	k	l
m	n	o	p
q	r	s	t
u	v	w	x
	y	z	

PICTORIAL ALPHABET.

A

a　　Ax

B

b　　Boy

C

c　　Cat

D

d　　Dog

E

e　　Elk

F

f　　Fox

G

g　　Girl

H

h　　Hen

I **i** Ink	**J** **j** Jug
K **k** Kid	**L** **l** Lark
M **m** Man	**N** **n** Nut
O **o** Ox	**P** **p** Pig
Q **q** Quail	**R** **r** Rat

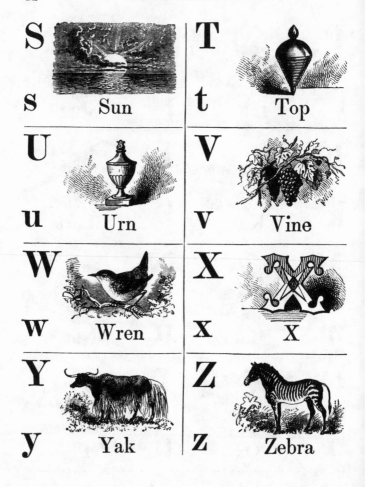

S s	Sun	T t	Top
U u	Urn	V v	Vine
W w	Wren	X x	X
Y y	Yak	Z z	Zebra

1 2 3 4 5 6 7 8 9 0

ECLECTIC SPELLING-BOOK.

Lesson 1.

SHORT SOUNDS OF VOWELS.

Short Sound of A.

ăm	eăt	gāp	băn	eăp
ăn	băd	băḡ	eăn	măp
ăṣ	măd	gāg	făn	năp
ăt	păd	hāḡ	păn	răp
ăx	săd	lăḡ	răn	hăp
răt	gād	tăḡ	tăn	jăm
săt	săp	făḡ	văn	hăm

Short Sound of E.

bĕd	dĕn	nĕt	sĕll	tĕnt
lĕd	kĕn	pĕt	nĕst	rĕnt
rĕd	mĕn	sĕt	zĕst	sĕnt
wĕd	wĕn	yĕt	tĕst	wĕnt
bĕḡ	jĕt	sĕx	pĕst	fĕlt
lĕḡ	lĕt	fĕll	rĕst	pĕlt
hĕn	mĕt	bĕll	jĕst	mĕlt

(13)

Lesson 2.

SHORT SOUNDS OF VOWELS.—Continued.

Short Sound of I.

ĭf	rĭd	hĭm	sĭn	jĭḡ
ĭt	lĭd	rĭm	tĭn	rĭḡ
ĭş	sĭp	fĭx	dĭḡ	bĭb
bĭt	tĭp	sĭx	fĭḡ	jĭb
hĭt	nĭp	dĭn	bĭḡ	rĭb
sĭt	lĭp	pĭn	pĭḡ	fĭb

Short Sound of O.

ŏn	ċŏb	nŏd	bŏx	dŏt
ŏx	jŏb	pŏd	hŏp	jŏt
ḡŏt	rŏb	rŏd	mŏp	lŏt
ċŏt	sŏb	lŏḡ	sŏp	pŏt
jŏt	ċŏd	hŏḡ	pŏp	rŏt
lŏt	Gŏd	dŏḡ	tŏp	nŏt

Short Sound of U.

ŭp	mŭd	rŭm	rŭt	ḡŭsh
ŭs	dŭḡ	sŭm	hŭng	dŭst
ċŭb	mŭḡ	bŭn	bŭng	mŭst
hŭb	pŭḡ	dŭn	lŭng	rŭst
rŭb	tŭḡ	rŭn	sŭng	ḡŭst
bŭd	jŭḡ	sŭn	hŭlk	drŭm

Lesson 3.

REVIEW OF SHORT SOUNDS OF VOWELS.

măn	lăp	păt	tăp	hăd
fĭn	gĕt	tĕn	wĕt	pĕg
fĭt	dĭm	mĭx	hĭd	hĭṣ
hŏt	rŏt	fŏb	dŏt	eŏn
rŭg	hŭm	fŭn	hŭt	eŭt
băd	fŭn	hŭg	gŭm	flŏg
dĕn	fŏg	dĭp	năg	drăm
dĭd	tŭb	fŏg	bĕt	hĕlp
sŏd	hŏd	gŭn	pĕn	lĭft
lăd	bĕt	dĭd	eŏg	rŭsh

Lesson 4.

Long Sound of A.

dāte	jāde	eāme	eāġe	bāne
lāte	fāde	dāme	pāġe	lāçe
māte	rāte	sāme	sāġe	wāke

Long Sound of E.

mē	wē	shē	hēed	wēed
fēe	jēer	fēed	dēed	dēep
fēel	lēer	mēek	kēep	pēep
sēek	vēer	bēef	rēel	wēep

Long Sound of I.

pīle	dīke	fīre	līfe	bīde
fīle	līke	tīre	rīfe	hīde
mīle	pīke	sīre	wīfe	rīde

Long Sound of O.

eōde	dōlt	bōne	hōpe	dōte
nōde	jōlt	eōne	pōpe	nōte
bōde	mōlt	hōne	rōpe	vōte
rōve	bōlt	tōne	eōpe	hōld

Long Sound of U.

lūre	eūbe	mūte	lūne	hūġe
eūre	tūbe	dūke	dūne	pūle
pūre	lūte	jūte	ūṣe	eūe

Lesson 5.

Short Sounds of Vowels.

erăb	blĕd	chĭp	shŏt	bŭmp
ḡrăb	flĕd	shĭp	blŏt	lŭmp
drăb	slĕd	whĭp	spŏt	pŭmp
slăb	spĕd	slĭp	plŏt	jŭmp
stăb	thĕn	drĭp	trŏt	hŭmp
brăḡ	bĕnt	spĭt	elŏḡ	bŭlk
erăm	bĕst	erĭb	frŏḡ	jŭst
elăn	hĕmp	ḡĭft	plŏd	drŭḡ
elăd	vĕst	kĭng	stŏp	shŭt
dăsh	wĕst	ḡrĭt	elŏd	hŭsh

Lesson 6.

Various Vowel Sounds.

bärd	dēạl	tănk	dĕll	ĭll
eärd	vēạl	rănk	tĕll	bĭll
härd	mēạl	sănk	wĕll	fĭll
bärk	nēạt	hănk	yĕll	rĭll
därk	hēạt	dănk	bĕlt	hĭll
dĭnt	băng	dimé	rāvé	eŭll
hĭnt	făng	limé	ḡāvé	dŭll
lĭnt	ḡăng	tīné	lāvé	ḡŭll
mĭnt	hăng	fīné	pāvé	hŭll
tĭnt	răng	mīné	sāvé	mŭll

Lesson 7.

Long Sounds of Vowels.

blāzé	snēer	drīvé	glōbé	dēản
erāzé	ereed	trībé	drōné	bēản
shāpé	stēep	brīné	stōné	bēảd
stāté	slēek	spīré	prōbé	bēảm
erāpé	flēet	brīdé	shōré	lēản
fūmé	smīté	blāmé	elēảr	mōpé
spūmé	spīté	flāmé	drēảr	mōld
flūké	quīté	slāté	blēảr	tōré
flūmé	whīné	spādé	spēảr	rōbé
dūré	spīné	prāté	smēảr	pōké

Lesson 8.

Various Sounds of Vowels.

elȧsp	small	erămp	brĭng	mōản
grȧsp	stall	stămp	elĭng	eōảst
flȧsk	fall	grănd	slĭng	tōảst
grȧft	wall	stănd	swĭng	rōảst
erȧft	squall	lămp	thĭng	rōảch
bôŏk	bōōn	stôrk	wạd	pŏd
gŏŏd	spōōn	hôrsé	wạs	rŏb
tŏŏk	blōōm	snôrt	wạsh	rŏck
fŏŏt	brōōm	shôrt	wạst	sŏft
hŏŏk	stōōl	nôrth	whạt	lŏst

Lesson 9.

Long Sounds of Vowels under the Accent.

fā'tal	lē'ḡal	lō'ᴄal	ᴄū'bit
nā'tal	rē'ḡal	fō'ᴄal	dū'el
pā'pal	rē'al	vō'ᴄal	hū'man
pā'ḡan	pē'nal	ō'ral	ū'nit
bā'by	tā'per	ō'val	dū'ly
lā'dy	dī'al	tō'tal	fū'ry
lā'zy	trī'al	bō'ny	jū'ry
mā'zy	fī'nal	ᴄō'ny	pū'ny
nā'vy	vī'tal	ḡō'ry	pū'pil
rā'çy	rī'val	rō'şy	hū'mid
Sā'tan	vī'al	pō'şy	tū'mid

Lesson 10.

Short Sounds of Vowels under the Accent.

ăl'um	ĕl'der	çĭv'il	ᴄŭl'prit
ăl'to	hĕe'tiᴄ	dĭt'ty	ᴄlŭm'şy
ᴄăn'ter	hĕlm'et	ḡĭd'dy	dŭl'çet
măr'ry	fĕn'nel	fĭl'ly	fŭn'nel
răl'ly	kĕn'nel	sĭl'ly	ḡŭl'ly
năp'kin	bĕl'fry	lĭv'id	bŭck'et
hăp'py	ĕd'dy	lĭm'it	ḡŭs'set
păn'try	ĕn'try	lĭm'ber	sŭl'len
răm'mer	ĕn'vy	rĭv'et	sŭm'mon
măm'mon	tĕst'y	lĭn'en	hŭr'ry
tăb'let	sĕlf'ish	mĭl'let	mŭl'let

Lesson 11.

Various Sounds of A.

eâré	fȧst	chärm	eămp	wạr
mâré	mȧst	chärt	dămp	wạrp
shâré	eȧsk	lärd	hănd	wạrm
spâré	mȧsk	ärm	lănd	wạrd
snâré	pȧst	yärd	sănd	wạrn
ḡāmé	seär	lāké	wȧft	frāẏ
lāmé	spär	dālé	rȧft	plāẏ
nāmé	stär	ḡālé	chȧff	ḡrāẏ
fāmé	ḡärb	eāpé	ȧft	stāẏ
tāmé	bärb	shāmé	stȧff	brāẏ

Lesson 12.

Various Sounds of A.

dăn′ḡer	ăm′ber	lärd′er	elăt′ter
măn′ḡer	băn′ter	mär′ḡin	flăt′ter
quāk′er	băn′ner	är′dent	lăt′ter
quā′ver	hănd′y	är′my	măt′ter
drā′per	măn′nȧ	ärt′ist	păt′ter
wā′ḡer	eăn′çer	här′vest	tăt′ter
fā′vor	păn′der	pär′ty	răḡ′ḡed
flā′vor	tăm′per	tär′dy	răck′et
sā′vor	plăn′et	är′dor	văn′ish
mā′jor	hăm′per	eär′pet	ḡăl′lant
eā′per	stăm′mer	ḡär′ment	păt′tern

Lesson 13.

Various Sounds of E.

shēep	çē'dar	bĕt'ter	elẽr'ġy
ereep	fē'ver	fĕt'ter	fẽr'vor
slēep	trē'mor	lĕt'ter	hẽr'mit
swēep	ġē'nus	ĕn'ter	mẽr'çy
spēed	sē'eret	ĕv'er	sẽr'mon
brēezę	rē'bus	nĕv'er	sẽr'pent
tēeth	sē'quel	sĕv'er	mẽr'chant
snēezę	sē'quençę	dĕx'ter	vẽr'bal
brēed	hē'ro	mĕm'ber	vẽr'diet
blēed	zē'ro	plĕn'ty	pẽr'sǿn
frēed	sē'eant	vĕn'om	fẽr'ment

Lesson 14.

Various Sounds of I.

bīrd	brī'er	bĭb'ber	thĩr'ty
bīrch	çī'der	bĭt'ter	thĩrst'y
chīrp	mī'ṣer	dif'fer	thĩrd'ly
flīrt	spī'der	dĭn'ner	bĩrch'ęn
ġīrl	vī'per	frĭt'ter	chĩrp'er
shīrt	elī'ent	lĭt'ter	ġĩrl'ish
squīrm	ġī'ant	rĭv'er	ġĩrd'er
squīrt	ī'tem	shĭv'er	stĩr'less
thīrd	ī'çy	sĭl'ver	fĩrst'ly
ġīrt	spī'ral	ĭn'ner	bĩrth'dāẏ
ġīrd	ī'vy	lĭv'er	mĩrth'ful

Lesson 15.

Various Sounds of O.

brō'ker	eŏl'ie	eôr'net	wõrst
elō'ver	tŏn'ie	eôr'set	eŏmₑ
drōv'er	tŏp'ie	ôr'ḡan	lŏvₑ
ḡrō'çer	mŏr'al	sôr'did	dŏvₑ
ō'ver	eŏm'mȧ	tôr'pid	shōōt
ō'dor	dŏḡ'ḡed	fôrm'al	mōōn
sō'lar	dŏe'tor	fôr'ty	mōōsₑ
pō'lar	eŏp'per	lôrd'ly	tōōth
pōk'er	fŏd'der	môrn'ing	ḡôrḡₑ
hōmₑ'ly	fŏs'ter	ôrb'it	mōst
pō'em	pŏn'der	môr'tal	prŏp

Lesson 16.

Various Sounds of U.

hū'mor	bŭt'ter	mûr'der	pru̟'dent
jū'ror	mŭt'ter	mûr'mur	fru̟'ḡal
tū'mor	rŭd'der	tûr'ban	tru̟'ly
stū'por	shŭt'ter	tûr'nip	tru̟'ant
tū'tor	sŭf'fer	tûr'kₑy	eru̟'et
eū'ratₑ	sŭp'per	pûr'pōrt	bru̟'in
lū'çid	mŭm'my	eûrl'y	dru̟'id
stū'dent	mŭs'ket	fûr'ry	ru̟'in
s̩tū'pid	nŭm'ber	fûr'nish	ru̟'by
lū'nar	nŭt'mĕḡ	eûr'vet	bru̟'tal
tū'mult	stŭt'ter	bûr'dₑn	ḡru̟'el

Lesson 17.

Various Sounds of the Vowels.

Jūne	fûrl	hŭsk	frŏm	hạlt
dūpe	hûrl	mŭsk	pŏmp	mạlt
tūne	tûrn	rŭsk	rŏmp	sạlt
flūte	chûrn	stŭng	lŏng	wạltz
plŭme	hûrt	plŭck	sŏng	swạn
ḡlue	eûrl	drŭṉk	strŏng	wạsp
drōop	dĕck	chĭll	fôr	shēạth
ḡlōom	nĕck	drĭll	eôrn	shĕll
lōop	nĕxt	quĭll	fôrk	shōrn
hōof	tĕxt	skĭll	fôrm	shout
rōof	dĕsk	spĭll	sôrt	shrŭb
prōof	nĕst	frĭll	tôrch	shrŭḡ

Lesson 18.

Words Accented on the last Syllable.

a wāke̸′	be hĕst′	be hīnd′	re çēde̸′
be ea̅me̸′	be sĕt′	be sīde̸′	eon erēte̸′
be hāve̸′	ea dĕt′	be tīde̸′	eom pēte̸′
be tāke̸′	de fĕnd′	de rīve̸′	se erēte̸′
e lāte̸′	de pĕnd′	re çīte̸′	eon çēde̸′
per vāde̸′	re pĕl′	re tīre̸′	eon vēne̸′
for sāke̸′	at tĕnd′	re vīle̸′	im pēde̸′
a bāte̸′	eon sĕnt′	re mīṣe̸′	re plēte̸′
ere āte̸′	im pĕnd′	re vīve̸′	un sēen′
es tāte̸′	im pĕl′	eon nīve̸′	su prēme̸′
re lāte̸′	eom pĕl′	ex çīte̸′	re lēaṣe̸′

Lesson 19.

be rāte̸′	a bōde̸′	ex pīre̸′	a eūte̸′
a pāçe̸′	a lōne̸′	eon fīde̸′	a būṣe̸′
re bāte̸′	a tōne̸′	eon fīne̸′	eon fūṣe̸′
de bāte̸′	af förd′	eon spīre̸′	de dūçe̸′
de fāçe̸′	ea jōle̸′	po līte̸′	de lūde̸′
de fāme̸′	de pōṣe̸′	re elīne̸′	ma tūre̸′
se dāte̸′	eom pōṣe̸′	re fīne̸′	pol lūte̸′
eol lāte̸′	en förçe̸′	re pīne̸′	pro eūre̸′
re g̅āle̸′	en rōbe̸′	re quīre̸′	re būke̸′
em pāle̸′	ex plōre̸′	re spīre̸′	re dūçe̸′
en g̅āg̅e̸′	ex pōṣe̸′	ū nīte̸′	se elūde̸′
en rāg̅e̸′	im pört′	en twīne̸′	se eūre̸′

Lesson 20.

blādé	plăsh	brĕ̇am	drĕss	twĭnĝ
ḡlādé	ɛlăsh	ɛrĕ̇am	swĕll	blīnd
ḡrādé	ɛrăsh	drĕ̇am	spĕnd	ḡrīnd
shādé	smăsh	ḡlĕ̇am	spĕck	spīké
trādé	trăsh	stĕ̇am	frĕsh	smīlé
skāté	slăsh	strĕ̇am	whĕlp	whīlé
brĭsk	drōvé	blŭsh	chĕ̇ap	ɛärvé
quĭlt	ḡrōvé	flŭsh	pĕ̇ach	färçé
fĭlth	stōvé	slŭsh	tĕ̇ach	pärsé
pĭnch	ɛlōvé	brŭsh	rĕ̇ach	bärġé
flĭnch	smōté	ɛrŭsh	blĕ̇ach	lärġé
mĭnçé	stōré	thrŭsh	ḡlĕ̇an	snärl

Lesson 21.

ăb'bé̇y	rĕɛ'ord	pĭt'y	ɛōl'ter
ăb'bot	chĕck'er	dĭs'tant	fō'ɛus
ăt'om	ĕd'it	dĭn'ġy	ḡlō'ry
ăsh'eṣ	lĕv'el	dĭz'zy	lō'ɛust
ɛăp'tor	mĕth'od	fĭn'ish	mō'ment
ɛăr'rot	splĕn'did	ḡĭm'let	pō'tent
ɛăv'il	vĕs'per	spĭr'it	ɛō'ġent
chăp'ter	wĕst'ern	tĭm'id	dō'taġé
chăt'tel	bĕd'lam	pĭġ'ġin	nō'ted
făth'om	dĕs'pot	tĭn'sel	stōr'aġé
ḡăl'lon	rĕn'der	tĭp'pet	stō'ry
ḡăl'lop	tĕm'pest	wĭt'ness	prō'test

Lesson 22.

shāk℘	chōṣ℘	märch	pīn℘	oil
snāk℘	prōṣ℘	pärch	wĭld	moil
bāst℘	thōṣ℘	stärch	mĭld	℮oil
hāst℘	frōz℘	lärch	tĭl℘	foil
tāst℘	fōrç℘	lärk	slĭd℘	soil
pāst℘	pōrch	stärk	ḡlĭd℘	toil
bŭnch	brŏth	prĭṣm	spĕnt	boy
hŭnch	℮lŏth	sĭxth	fĕnç℘	℮oy
lŭnch	frŏth	stĭnt	hĕnç℘	hoy
pŭnch	mŏth	smĭth	pĕnç℘	joy
plŭmp	bŏ℘ch	whĭst	thĕnç℘	toy
stŭmp	stŏck	mĭdst	whĕnç℘	℮loy

Lesson 23.

Monosyllables miscellaneously arranged.

frēe	℮lĭp	shĕlf	quĕst	shīn℘
spĭn	hāt℘	chīd℘	flăx	wōr℘
shăd	tāp℘	frĭnḡ℘	stĭll	thĭnk
bănd	rāç℘	℮lŏck	trĭm	märsh
păck	mīr℘	chēek	dōor	bōoth
bāth	kīt℘	fu̇ll	℮lŭng	wĭnç℘
dŏck	bănk	frŏck	lŏft	sprāy̆
ḡōld	fĕll	trōop	pŭlp	join
pīp℘	pĭnk	ḡlȧss	ḡrāp℘	frĭz
℮lŭb	hĭlt	lûrk	pōṣ℘	brow
shŏp	lȧst	℮loud	zĕst	ḡrāç℘

Lesson 24.

Words in which the final *e* is silent.

ċā′blė	nēe′dlė	răb′blė	bŭb′blė
fā′blė	Bī′blė	săm′plė	bŭn′dlė
ḡā′blė	tī′tlė	sĭm′plė	ċrŭm′blė
sā′blė	rī′flė	tĕm′plė	mŭf′flė
stā′blė	nŏ′blė	dĭm′plė	mŭz′zlė
ċrā′dlė	fĭck′lė	fĭd′dlė	pŭd′dlė
lā′dlė	ăm′plė	kĭn′dlė	rŭf′flė
mā′plė	ăp′plė	lĭt′tlė	tŭm′blė
stā′plė	băf′flė	bŏt′tlė	pûr′plė
bēe′tlė	băt′tlė	ċŏb′blė	çīr′ċlė
fēe′blė	ċăt′tlė	fŏnd′lė	săd′dlė

Lesson 25.

ān′ġel	ăb′sent	bĭsh′op	blŭn′der
bā′sis	ăċ′rid	bĭḡ′ot	blŭs′ter
ċā′ter	blăṉk′et	bĭl′let	ċŭs′tom
flā′ḡrant	ċlăs′sie	blĭs′ter	ċŭt′ler
frā′ḡrant	ċrăḡ′ḡy	çĭn′der	ċŭt′ter
hăs′ty	dăm′şel	ċrĭck′et	sŭm′mer
hā′tred	dăṉ′dy	fĭf′ty	sŭn′der
lā′bel	făb′rie	fĭl′let	shŭd′der
pā′tent	făm′ish	lĭm′pid	thŭn′der
sā′ċred	frăn′tiċ	pĭl′fer	tŭm′bler
stātė′ment	lăth′er	pĭl′lar	ŭl′çer
vā′ċātė	lăv′ish	prĭnt′er	ŭn′der

Lesson 26.

DICTATION EXERCISES.

NOTE TO TEACHERS.—These lessons are intended as exercises in the *meaning* as well as the *spelling* of words. Distinguish carefully words of similar sound, but which differ in their spelling. At the recitation the sentences should be read aloud by the teacher, and the pupils required to write them out neatly and correctly upon their slates or on the blackboard.

He ate seven or eight apples. Send the pale maid with the pail of milk. He owed for the paper on which he wrote an ode to the moon. We are not quite ready for the quiet man. Age gives edge to wine. He said the idol looked like a satyr. Clever satire often rouses the idle.

Lesson 27.

Sounds of *ai, ou, ow,* and *ea.*

pāíd	bound	eow	cheạt	hĕạd
ḡrāín	found	how	treạt	dĕạd
stāíd	ḡround	town	bēạst	stĕạd
wāíf	hound	ḡrowl	bleạt	trĕạd
rāíl	mound	elown	preạch	dreạd
flāíl	pound	frown	speạk	thrĕạd
quāíl	round	erown	strēạk	sweạt
snāíl	sound	drown	fēạst	dĕạth

Lesson 28.

Dissyllables with short Sounds of Vowels.

ăd'agĕ	frĕn'zy	bĭck'er	blŏs'som
băl'last	ĕmp'ty	erĭt'ie	eŏt'tŏn
bănt'ling	g̣ĕn'try	dĭg̣'it	eŏm'ie
eăn'to	mĕr'it	flĭm'ṣy	drŏp'sy
răs'eal	mĕn'tal	flĭp'pant	flŏr'id
lăs'so	shĕr'iff	frĭg̣'id	frŏl'ie
ăn'tie	tĕn'dril	ĭn'fant	g̣ŏs'pel
săd'ness	vĕl'lum	ĭn'g̣ress	g̣ŏs'sip
săl'ver	vĕl'vet	ĭn'mātĕ	hŏr'rid
sănd'y	nĕe'tar	ĭn'quest	jŏl'ly
măg̣'g̣ot	vĕs'try	ĭn'seet	rŏck'et.

Lesson 29.

Trisyllables with short Sounds of the Vowels.

băl'eo ny	dĕl'i eatĕ	lĭb'er ātĕ
băr'o ny	dĕs'o latĕ	lĭm'i tātĕ
eăv'i ty	dĕr'o g̣ātĕ	ĭm'mo lātĕ
făe'ul ty	dĕv'as tātĕ	ĭn'di eātĕ
g̣răv'i ty	ĕm'ū lātĕ	ĭn'ti mātĕ
măl'a dy	hĕṣ'i tātĕ	ĭn'du rātĕ
văn'i ty	mĕd'i tātĕ	ĭn'vo eātĕ
ăm'pu tātĕ	pĕt'ri fȳ	ĭr'ri tātĕ
ăb'so lūtĕ	plĕn'i tūdĕ	lĭt'i g̣ātĕ
ăl'ti tūdĕ	rĕe'ti tūdĕ	mĭl'i tātĕ
ăm'bu lanᴄĕ	rĕṣ'o lūtĕ	stĭp'ū lātĕ

Lesson 30.

Miscellaneous Sounds.

primé	swing	straw	crawl
brawn	snoré	gloss	flänk
brick	chärgé	crow	quench
green	tingé	shärk	Seŏtch
chest	goosé	bränd	thrift
späçé	prow	twist	flängé
cränk	wĕalth	slíçé	twäin
limp	serew	throb	thríçé
chĕss	flāké	soon	flĕsh
finch	flăsh	flaw	twĕlvé
flŭng	clĕan	loaf	scālé

Lesson 31.

Long Sounds of I and U, and short Sounds of E and I.

a bīdé′	ac cūsé′	con tĕnd′	ad mĭt′
a līké′	im pūré′	con tĕnt′	ad dĭet′
a līvé′	im pūté′	in tĕnd′	as sĭst′
a rīsé′	as sūmé′	in tĕnt′	com mĭt′
de çīdé′	com mūté′	dis sĕet′	con sĭst′
de fīlé′	com mūné′	de jĕet′	de pĭet′
de fīné′	com pūté′	de tĕst′	dis tĭll′
de rīdé′	con clūdé′	de tĕet′	e mĭt′
de şīré′	con fūté′	in spĕet′	en lĭst′
dĭ vīdé′	dis pūté′	ob jĕet′	en rĭch′
dĭ vīné′	en dūré′	re spĕet′	for bĭd′

Lesson 32.

Silent Letters.

B is silent after *m* and before *t*, and *p* is silent before *s*. The silent letters are canceled in this lesson, as they are throughout the book.

lămb	nŭmb	dĕbt	dĕbt'or
ċōmb	bōmb	doubt	doubt'ful
tọmb	ċrŭmb	psäĺm	sŭb'tlė
dŭmb	thŭmb	pshaẃ	psạl'ter

DICTATION EXERCISES ON THE ABOVE.

The lamb is a dumb animal. He climbed the hill to the tomb, but his limbs became numb. Comb your hair, but do not thumb your book. Bombs are now commonly called "shells." The debtor, who was a subtle man, doubted his word, and gave not a crumb of comfort. Take your psalter and select a joyous psalm. His answer was, "Pshaw!"

Lesson 33.

Sounds of *igh*, *oa*, *shr*, and *thr*.

nīgh	lōad	ċōax	shrănk	thrăsh
thīgh	ōats	hōax	shrewd	thrĕat
fīght	bōat	ōath	shrift	thrŏng
līght	ōak	ċōach	shrīke	thrōve
flīght	fōal	flōat	shrŭnk	thrŭst
frīght	gōat	pōach	thrill	thrōat
tīght	sōap	hōarse	thrēe	thrŭm

Lesson 34.

Long and short Sounds of A, and short Sound of E.

gāi̯n	a băsh'	dis păt̯ch'	pre tĕnd'
nāi̯l	ea băl'	dis trăet'	re flĕet'
tāi̯nt	ea năl'	ex pănd'	re frĕsh'
trāi̯l	era văt'	a bĕt'	re lĕnt'
āi̯m	de eămp'	be dĕck'	re jĕet'
māi̯m	pro trăet'	be hĕld'	re quĕst'
trāi̯n	re eănt'	be quĕst'	re bĕl'
strāi̯n	re frăet'	de fĕet'	re ḡrĕss'
chāi̯n	re lăx'	e lĕet'	re prĕss'
pāi̯nt	at tăck'	e rĕet'	sub jĕet'
quāi̯nt	at trăet'	e vĕnt'	neḡ lĕet'

Lesson 35.

Short Sounds of Vowels under the Accent.

ăe'çi dent	bĕn'e fit	dĭf'fer ent
ăd'a mant	brĕv'i ty	dĭf'fi eult
ăm'i ty	elĕm'en çy	fĭl'a ment
ăn'i mal	dĕs'ti ny	ĭn'ere ment
ăn'nu al	nĕḡ'li ḡent	ĭn'do lent
eăn'is ter	pĕnd'ū lŭm	hĭs'to ry
flăt'ter y	rĕm'e dy	ĭn'ju ry
făm'i ly	rĕḡ'ū lar	pĭl'lo ry
lăx'i ty	rĕl'e vant	sĭm'i lar
măn'i fest	pĕn'i tençǿ	tĭt'ū lar
măn'i fōld	pĕn'e trātǿ	tĭm'or ǿŭs

Lesson 36.

SOUNDS OF THE VOWELS, DIPHTHONGS, AND CONSONANTS.

In this lesson, and in the pages immediately following, will be found forty-three exercises on the various sounds of the English language. Some of these have been given already, but are repeated here for the more thorough instruction of the pupil. Let the teacher carefully discriminate between the different sounds of the vowels, and fully drill the scholars in their correct enunciation.

1. Regular Long Sound of A, marked ā.

māke	lā'tent	brāve	a bāse'ment
sāfe	chăm'ber	erāve	a bāte'ment
gāze	pās'try	grāve	ad jā'çent
sāint	măn'ġy	shāve	a wā'ken

Lesson 37.

2. Regular Short Sound of A, marked ă.

spăn	ăd'der	erăck	eăn'di dāte
trăp	ăn'vil	ğlănd	eăl'i eo
plăt	băn'ish	slăck	ğrăt'i tūde
shăm	brăn'dy	plăid	măġ'is trāte

3. Sound of A before r in such words as *air*, *care*, marked â.

dâre	af fâir'	châir	trans pâr'ent
râre	de spâir'	prâyer	for bear'ançe
flâre	be wâre'	seâre	pâr'ent aġe
ğlâre	eom pâre'	squâre	eâre'ful ness

Sp. 3.

Lesson 38.

4. Sound of the Italian A, as in *arm*, marked ä.

färm	är′bor	g̣üärd	är′g̣u ment
härm	är′mor	däṵnt	är′ti chōk̸
bärn	bär′ber	härsh	ҽär′di nal
yärn	ҽär′g̣o	jäṵnt	ҽär′pen ter

5. Sound of A in certain words before *ff, ft, ss, st, sk, sp*, and in a few before *nce* and *nt*, marked à, as in *staff*.

màss	chànç̸	g̣àsp	chàn′çel lor
ҽlàss	pàss′pōrt	quàff	chàn′çer y
vàst	màs′ter	chànt	ҽràft′i ness
tàsk	g̣ràft′ed	prànç̸	ad vàn′tag̸̣

Lesson 39.

6. Sound of broad A, as in *all*, marked ạ.

thrạll	de bạṵch′	drạẉl	ạṵ′di enç̸
tạll	de fạṵlt′	pạẉn	lạṵd′a bl̸
wạrt	de frạṵd′	sprạẉl	plạṵṣ′i bl̸
ạẉ̸	as sạṵlt′	wạrmth	tạ/k′a tïv̸

7. Short Sound of broad A, as in *what*, marked ặ.

wạn	wạn′ton	squạsh	squạl′id ness
wạnd	wạn′der	squạb	wạsp′ish ly
squạt	squạn′der	squạd	wạ̧tch′ful ness
wạ̧tch	wạl′lōẉ	swạmp	whạt ĕv′er

Lesson 40.

8. Regular Long Sound of E, as in *eve*, marked ē.

fēel	fē′māl₡	wē₰n	dē′i ty
kēel	pēe′vish	thē§₡	dē′çen çy
ḡlēe	quē′ry	prį′est	e ḡrē′ḡįøŭs
dēem	nē₰′ther	chēer	frē′quen çy

9. Regular Short Sound of E, as in *end*, marked ĕ.

ĕbb	pĕn′ny	slĕḑḡ₡	ĕn′e my
frĕt	sĕe′ond	sprĕad	rĕe′og nīz₡
hĕlm	tĕn′der	ꞣnĕlt	lĕn′i ty
thĕm	rĕe′tor	elĕft	mĕm′o ry

Lesson 41.

10. Sound of E as in *there*, marked ê. This corresponds with the sound of *a* in *care*.

nê'er	pär têrre'	whêre up ŏn'
whêre	êre lŏng'	whêre un to'
thêre ŏf'	thêre bȳ'	whêre a bouts'
hêir'ess	whêre ăt'	whêre with al'

11. Sound of E like ā, as in *prey*, marked e̱.

the̱y	ne̱igh'bor	ne̱igh'bor hŏod
whe̱y	he̱i'nŏus	sur ve̱y'or
fre̱ight	o be̱y'	pur ve̱y'ançe
de̱ign	in ve̱igh'	con ve̱y'ançe

Lesson 42.

12. Sound of E before *r*, verging toward the sound of *u* in *urge*, and marked ẽ.

tẽrm	ẽr'mine	tẽrse	tẽr'ma ḡant
pẽarl	ẽar'ly	mẽrge	pẽr'son al
ẽrr	pẽr'feet	yẽarn	mẽr'chan dise
lẽarn	mẽr'çer	swẽrve	sẽr'mon īze

13. Regular Long Sound of I, as in *ice*, marked ī.

fīfe	dī'et	Christ	brīb'er y
crīme	quī'et	spīçe	dī'a dem
shrīne	fī'at	strīve	lī'a ble
thrīve	plī'ant	slime	ī'çi cle

Lesson 43.

14. Regular Short Sound of I, as in *ill*, marked ĭ.

stĭng	pĭv′ot	sprĭng	dĭf′fi dent
blĭss	splĭn′ter	twĭtch	pĭn′a fōrẹ
ĭnch	tĭn′der	thĭck	ĭn′fa my
strĭp	wĭck′ed	sphĭṉx	lĭt′ur ġy

15. Sound of I like that of long ē, as in *pique*, marked ī.

pe tītẹ′	fa tīḡụẹ′	măḡ a zīnẹ′
an tïqụẹ′	in trīḡụẹ′	sŭb ma rīnẹ′
ea prïçẹ′	po lïçẹ′	vēr′di ḡrïs
fas çïnẹ′	va lïsẹ′	quạr′an tïnẹ

Lesson 44.

16. Sound of I before *r*, verging toward *u* in *urge*, marked ï.

stïr	bïrth′rīg̸ht	ḡïrth	ḡïrl′ish ness
fïrst	ḡïrd′lẹ	thïrst	mïrth′ful ness
fïrm	ïrk′sȯmẹ	fïrth	thïr′ti eth
skïrt	vïr′ġin	smïrch	flïrt′ing ly

17. Regular Long Sound of O, as in *old*, marked ō.

hōst	pō′et	e̸hrōmẹ	fō′lĭ o
smōkẹ	tō′ry	blōẘn	ḡlō′ri fȳ
spōrt	lō′eātẹ	seōld	ō′pi atẹ
slōpẹ	sō′lō	drōll	pō′et ry

Lesson 45.

18. Regular Short Sound of O, as in *not*, marked ŏ.

bŏnd	mŏn'ster	croft	lŏn'ġi tūde
frŏst	pŏt'ter	seŏnçe	prŏmpt'i tūde
lŏdġe	lŏdġ'ment	mŏsque	nŏm'i nāte
prŏng	yŏn'der	frŏnd	ŏb'li ḡāte

19. Sound of O like short *u*, as in *dove*, marked ȯ.

mȯnth	blȯod'shĕd	spȯnġe	cȯv'ert ly
ḡlȯve	lȯve'ly	tȯngue	cȯv'e nant
shȯve	nȯth'ing	flȯod	brȯth'er hŏod
frȯnt	cȯv'et	blȯod	mȯth'er lў

Lesson 46.

20. Sound of O like ōō long, as in *do*, marked ǫ.

whǫm	tǫur'ist	ḡrǫup	whǫ ĕv'er
mǫve	rǫu tïne'	prǫve	shǫe'-māk er
tǫur	thrǫugh out'	dǫuçhe	en tǫmb'ment
shǫe	en tǫmb'	yǫuth	mǫv'ing ly

21. Sound of O like ŏŏ short, as in *wolf*, marked ǫ.

wǫlf	bǫ'ṣom	em bǫ'ṣom	wǫl ver ēne'
wǫuld	wǫm'an	un bǫ'ṣom	wǫm'an ly
cǫuld	wǫlf'ish	wǫm'an hŏod	wǫm'an ish
shǫuld	wǫlf'-nĕt	wǫrst'ed	wǫlf'ish ly

Lesson 47.

22. Sound of O like ą (broad *a*), as in *form*, marked ô.

bôrn	tôrt'ūr¢	€ôrps¢	fôrm'al ĭst
hôrn	fôrk'ed	thôrn	€ôr'mo rant
môrs¢	fôr'mer	seôrn	hôr'ta tĭv¢
lôrn	fôr'ward	seôrch	môr'ti fȳ

23. Another mark has been added in this book to indicate a sound of O where it precedes *r*, as in *work*, marked õ.

wõrk	wõr'thy	wõrs¢	wõr'thi lў
wõrd	wõr'ship	wõrld	wõrld'li ness
wõrm	ĕf'fõrt	whõrl	wõr'ship er
wõrt	wõrld'ly	whõrt	wõrk'ing-măn

Lesson 48.

24. Regular Long Sound of double O, as in *moon*, marked ōō.

tōōl	mōōn'shīn¢	ḡrōōm	bōōr'ish ness
nōōn	nōōn'tīd¢	se}͞ool	ḡlōōm'i ly
spōōl	blōōm'ing	sōōth¢	rōōm'i ness
ḡrōōv¢	ḡlōōm'y	smōōth	sōōth'sāy ing

25. Regular Short Sound of double O, as in *wool*, marked ŏŏ.

wŏŏl	hŏŏd'wink	brŏŏk	€ŏŏp'er ag¢
lŏŏk	lŏŏk'out	€rŏŏk	rŏŏk'er y
rŏŏk	wŏŏd'land	shŏŏk	bŏŏk'-bind er
hŏŏd	wŏŏl'ly	stŏŏd	€rŏŏk'ed ness

Lesson 49.

26. Regular Long Sound of U, as in *mute*. marked ū.

sūe	be̸aū'ty	deūçe̸	be̸aū'ti ful
lie̸ū	fe̸ūd'al	slūi̧çe̸	eū'ti ele̸
nūde̸	eū'bie	jūi̧çe̸	mū'ti ny
sūi̧t	flū'id	fūḡu̧e̸	pū'ri ty

27. Regular Short Sound of U, as in *but*, marked ŭ.

lŭngṣ	slŭm'ber	elŭmp	bŭt'ter y
plŭsh	rŭs'set	stŭnt	eŭs'to dy
dŭnçe̸	dŭch'ess	skŭlk	lŭx'ū ry
trŭmp	seŭf'fle̸	yőŭng	sŭm'ma ry

Lesson 50.

28. Sound of U when preceded by *r* in the same syllable, as in *rude*, marked u̧. It is the same sound as ōō.

tru̧e̸	ru̧'mor	pru̧ne̸	eru̧'di ty
eru̧de̸	ru̧'ral	tru̧çe̸	rḩe̸u̧'ma tĭṣm
eru̧se̸	tru̧f'fle̸	spru̧çe̸	pru̧'dent ly
ru̧le̸	bru̧'tish	eru̧i̧ṣe̸	pru̧'ri ent

29. Sound of U like that of short ŏŏ, as in *put*, marked u̧.

bu̧ll	pu̧l'pit	fu̧l'ly	fu̧l fĭll'ment
pu̧ll	pu̧l'le̸y	bu̧sh'y	bu̧l'le tin
pu̧t	eu̧sh'i̧on	pu̧ss'y	bu̧ll'ion ist
pu̧sh	bu̧l'wark	bu̧t̸ch'er	bu̧sh'i ness

Lesson 51.

30. Sound of U before *r* in such words as *urge*, marked û.

ûrġȩ	jȯûr′nȩy	spûrn	ûr′ġen çy
bûrn	stûr′ġȩòn	nûrsȩ	ȩûrl′i ness
spûr	chûrch′man	ȩûrst	jȯûr′nal ĭst
ȩûrb	bûr′ġess	bûrst	hûrt′fu̟l ness

31. Regular Long Sound of Y, as in *fly*, marked ȳ.

ap plȳ′	tȳ′rant	pȳrȩ	dȳ′nas ty
de nȳ′	hȳ′drà	tȳpȩ	ăn′tĭ tȳpȩ
re lȳ′	tȳ′phus	fȳkȩ	a sȳ′lum
re plȳ′	tȳ′rō	ȩẖȳmȩ	hy ē′nà

Lesson 52.

32. Regular Short Sound of Y, as in *hymn*, marked ў.

pўx	sўs′tem	lўmph	sўm′me try
çўst	sўn′tax	nўmph	sўn̠′ȩō pe
tўmp	phўṣ′iȩ	trўst	sўn′diȩ atȩ
Stўx	lўr′iȩ	rўnd	syn ŏp′sis

33. The sound of *oi* or *oy* (unmarked), as heard in *oil*, *oyster*.

oint	re ȩoil′	spoil	en joy′ment
voiçȩ	re joiçȩ′	moist	dis joint′ed
troy	de stroy′	broil	em ploy′ment
poiṣȩ	em ploy′	choiçȩ	ap point′ment

Lesson 53.

34. The sound of *ow* (unmarked), as heard in *owl*. When the *ow* is sounded as in *blown*, the *o* is marked long (blōwn).

howl	al low'	ᴄrowd	flow'er y
ḡown	en dow'	prowl	pow'er fu̇l
ᴄowl	vow'el	sᴄowl	em bow'el
down	row'el	brown	en dow'ment

35. The diphthong *ou* has two leading sounds: that of *ow* in words derived from the Anglo-Saxon, as in *out;* and that of ōō in words derived from the French, as in *soup*.

sour	found'ling	fount	an nounçe̸'ment
pout	ḡround'less	mount	un found'ed
so̟u̸p	ro̸u̸ lett̸e̸'	ᴄro̸u̸p	ᴄro̸u̸'pĭ er
ro̟u̸p	ḡro̸u̸p'ing	wo̟u̸nd	tro̟u̸'ba do̸u̸r

Lesson 54.

36. The consonant C has two regular sounds: as soft *c* in *cede*, marked ç; as hard *c* in *cot*, where it has the sound of *k*, and is marked ᴄ.

çīv̸e̸ṣ	ăç'id	trāç̸e̸	De çĕm'ber
māç̸e̸	sŏl'aç̸e̸	brāç̸e̸	in çĕs'sant
ᴄlŏt	tă̇e'tiᴄ	ᴄûrd	en ăᴄt'ment
ăᴄts	trăf'fiᴄ	ᴄāv̸e̸	e lĕᴄt'or

37. The sound of N as heard in *link*, is marked thus, ṉ, which is the same sound as that represented by *ng*.

lăṉk	mŏṉk'e̸y	drĭṉk	ᴄŏṉ'ḡru̟ ø̸ŭs
mŏṉk	ᴄŏṉ'ḡress	trŭṉk	sĭṉ'ḡu lar
sŭṉk	lăṉ'ḡuaḡ̸e̸	ᴄŏṉeᴋ̸	drŭṉk'e̸n ness

Lesson 55.

38. S has two regular sounds: when unmarked it has its
sharp or hissing sound, as in *yes;* when marked thus, ş, it has
the buzzing sound of *z* in *zeal.*

sĭck	măss'y	smĕlt	pos sĕss'ĭvĕ
pĕst	vĕst'ment	grōss	as sĕss'or
hăş	a mūşĕ'	grōẉş	re şĕm'blĕ
ēạşĕ	in fūşĕ'	ruşĕ	rĕş'o nant

39. Ch has three sounds: unmarked (English *ch*), it has
nearly the sound of *tsh,* as in *child;* marked thus, çh (French
ch), it has the sound of *sh,* as in *chaise;* and marked thus, ᴄh
(Latin *ch*), it has the sound of *k,* as in *chorus.*

sŭch	spēech'less	chĭld	chŏᴄ'o latĕ
çhĕf	ma çhĭnĕ'	çhāị̈şĕ	çhĭv'al rẏ
ᴄḥăşm	ᴄḥĕm'ist	ᴄḥrĭşm	ᴄḥăr'aᴄ ter

Lesson 56.

40. G has two regular sounds: marked thus, ḡ (*g* hard), it
has the sound of *g* in *go;* marked thus, ġ (*g* soft), it has the
compound sound of *j,* as in *gem.*

ḡeạr'ing	ḡew'ḡaẉ	slŭḡ	ḡĭd'di ness
ġen'tilĕ	slŭḡ'ḡish	ᴄrăḡ	ḡụ̈íl'lo tĭnĕ
ġĕn'der	ġĕst'ūrĕ	ġībĕ	ġĕn'er al

41. Th has two sounds: its sharp sound, as in *thing,* which is
unmarked, and its soft sound, as in *thine,* marked th.

thĭn	thē'ist	brĕạth	mẏth'iᴄ al
thaẉ	thē'sis	thĕft	thē'o ry
thĭs	ḡăth'er	thĭnĕ	hĭth'er tọ
thăn	bŏth'er	brēạthĕ	ȯth'er wĭşĕ

Lesson 57.

42. X has three sounds: its regular sharp sound (unmarked) like *ks*, as in *expect*, and its soft or flat sound like *gz*, as in *exist*, marked x̱. At the beginning of words *x* has the sound of *z*, as in *xebec* (zē′bec).

ĕx′it	ex păn′sĭv∉	ex trā′ne ∉ŭs
ex çĕl′	ĕx′pi āt∉	ex tē′ri or
ex̱ a̱lt′	ex̱ ăm′pl∉	ex̱ ĕe′ū tĭv∉
ex̱ ĕmpt′	ex̱ ŭlt′ant	ex̱ ôr′di ŭm

43. Q is followed in all cases by *u*, and has usually the sound of *kw*, as in *queen*; but in a few words derived from the French, *qu* is sounded like *k*, as in *coquette*.

quăck	quēer′ly	quoit	quī ē′tus
quēen	quō′rum	quōt∉	quo tā′tion
plăqu∉	pĭqu̷′ant	bĭsqu∉	eo qu̷ĕt′tish
elïqu̷∉	eo qu̷ĕt′	tôrqu̷∉	pĭqu̷′an çy

Lesson 58.

eas eād∉′	a bās∉′	in elūd∉′	a lärm′
ex chānġ∉′	a māz∉′	ad jūr∉′	a fär′
in flăm∉′	a brād∉′	de pūt∉′	re märk′
ob lāt∉′	eru sād∉′	re fūs∉′	de bärk′
par tāk∉′	de bās∉′	ma nūr∉′	em bärk′
ad drĕss′	re ḡrĕt′	in jĕet′	ae quĭt′
re flĕx′	ex çĕpt′	in vĕnt′	a drĭft′
ar rĕst′	ex pĕet′	mo lĕst′	re mĭss′
eon tĕst′	ex pĕnd′	op prĕss′	be fĭt′
de prĕss′	ex prĕss′	re drĕss′	per sĭst′

Lesson 59.

HOMOPHONOUS WORDS.

Note.—These exercises on words of similar sound, instead of being gathered into a single department, are interspersed throughout the book.

rāịṣḙd, *lifted up.*
rāzḙd, *destroyed.*
prīḛ̣ṣ, *inspects closely.*
prīzḙ, *to value.*
prāy̧, *to supplicate.*
prẹy̧, *a spoil.*
pōrḙ, *a small opening.*
pōụr, *to cause to flow.*
pōll, *the head.*
pōlḙ, *a rod; a perch.*

plāịt, *a fold.*
plātḙ, *flattened metal.*
plŭmḅ, *perpendicular.*
plŭm, *a fruit.*
plāçḙ, *site; spot.*
plāịçḙ, *a fish.*
plēạṣḙ, *to gratify.*
plēạṣ, *excuses.*
bĕll, *a sounding vessel.*
bĕllḙ, *a fine young lady.*

Lesson 60.

bīgḩt, *a bay.*
bītḙ, *to seize with the teeth.*
blōạt, *to swell.*
blōtḙ, *to dry and smoke.*
bōạrd, *a plank.*
bōrḙd, *did bore.*
brĕạd, *food.*
brĕd, *reared.*
blūḙ, *a color.*
blew, *did blow.*
bōạr, *the male swine.*
bōrḙ, *to pierce.*

pịēçḙ, *a part.*
pēạçḙ, *quietness.*
new, *not old.*
ḵnew, *did know.*
ǵnū, *a quadruped.*
lĭmḅ, *a branch.*
lĭmṋ, *to draw or paint.*
äre, *part of a circle.*
ärk, *a vessel.*
prāy̧ṣ, *supplicates.*
prāịṣḙ, *honor.*
prẹy̧ṣ, *spoils.*

Lesson 61.

Words accented on the last Syllable.

ab rŭpt′	dis ̄euss′	a ̄erŏss′	a ḡrēe′
an nŭl′	de dŭet′	a dŏpt′	a slēep′
̄eon strŭet′	in dŭet′	a lŏft′	es tēem′
in strŭet′	re bŭt′	a nŏn′	de ̄erēe
in trŭst′	re ṣŭlt′	be lŏng′	de ḡrēe′
at tīrę′	in vītę′	̄eom pŏrt′	dis ̄elōṣę′
en tīçę′	o blīġę′	re pŏrt′	dis pōṣę′
en tīrę′	per spīrę′	̄eon sōlę′	re stōrę′
in ̄elīnę′	sub līmę′	re pōṣę′	en thrōnę′
in çītę′	sur vīvę′	̄eon vōkę′	ex plōdę′

Lesson 62.

DICTATION EXERCISES.

Dost consider that dust thou art? He paid
the servant his hire, and the wages were
higher than last year. With whoop and
hurra they tore the hoop from the barrel.
The mower will cut more grass to-morrow.
The foreign consul took counsel with the
enemy, and called a council of war. English
consols are high. Kings are sometimes guilty
of flagrant wrongs. Many a fragrant flower
blooms unseen. He tore his clothes in a
struggle to close the door. His course toward
that coarse lad was wrong.

Lesson 63.

Words accented on the first Syllable.

eŏn'taet	nŏs'tril	eŭr'ry	pŭn'ġent
fŏr'est	prŏd'uet	fŭl'erum	rŭs'tie
hŏb'by	prŏb'lem	hŭd'dlĕ	rŭb'bish
lŏft'y	rŏs'ter	pŭb'lie	sŭlk'y
lŏġ'ie	tŏr'rent	pŭb'lish	sŭl'try
ăf'flux	băṉk'rupt	kĭn'dred	serĭb'blĕ
ăm'bush	eăm'phor	pĭck'et	trĭp'let
ăn'them	hăv'oe	tĭck'et	trĭck'lĕ
ăn'nalṣ	hăġ'ġard	wĭck'et	lĭz'ard
ăs'peet	hătch'et	ĭn'voiçĕ	vĭl'là

Lesson 64.

eam'brie	dē'ist	çȳ'press	trīb'al
eā'dençe	ē'qual	Frī'dȧў̃	erī'sis
dā'tĭve	frēe'dom	īçe'bẽrg̃	hȳ'drant
nā'tĭve	nēed'fụl	lī'bel	sçī'ençe
pāve'ment	mēet'ing	mī'grāte	sī'lent

dūke'dȯm	boun'ty	pow'der	boy'hŏŏd
dūr'ançe	eoun'ty	prow'ess	elois'ter
eū'beb	eow'ard	sound'ingṣ	joy'ọus
pū'trid	drow'ṣy	tow'el	loi'ter
pūr'ist	fount'ȧin	tow'er	loy'al

Lesson 65.

bē̇ard	bụild	päl̇m	vẽrse	wĭt̆ch
erēaṣe	bụilt	eäl̇f	sēȧrch	seript
ēaveṣ	squĭnt	häl̇f	fẽrn	g̃ụĕss
hēave	lĭve	ta̤l̇k	kẽrn	stärt
lēap	stĭck	wa̤l̇k	spẽrm	ẉräth
ḳnēe	eliff	cha̤l̇k	sẽrve	flōor
splēen	ẉrĭt	la̤ẉn	wẽre	çzär
hăve	brŏnze	da̤ụb	l̇ẽrb	häụnch
fră̱nk	bŭzz	fa̤ụlt̤	strĕngth	fläụnt
slāke	snăt̆ch	spaẉn	snēa̱k	häụnt
smăck	drĕd̆ge	drĭft	pûrse	shärp
elămp	chûrch	fŭnd	elŭt̆ch	ḳnēel

Lesson 66.

en nō'blǝ	in dūçǝ'ment	a bŭ'sĭvǝ
e lōpǝ'ment	a ɛū'men	pe ru̬'ṣal
ex pō'nent	aɛ ɛū'ṣant	pur sū'ant
he rō'iɛ	al lūrǝ'ment	re fūṣ'al
pro mō'tĭvǝ	a mūṣǝ'ment	sul phū'riɛ
de tăch'ment	es tăb'lish	at tĕnd'ant
doḡ măt'iɛ	fa năt'iɛ	as sĕm'blaḡǝ
dra măt'iɛ	fan tăs'tiɛ	ap pĕnd'ant
eɛ stăt'iɛ	ḡī ḡăn'tiɛ	in tĕs'tatǝ
e lăs'tiɛ	in hăb'it	ɛŏm'pen sātǝ

Lesson 67.

çĭt, *a citizen.*
sĭt, *to rest on a seat.*
dŭet, *a channel.*
dŭckǝd, *plunged under.*
chŭff, *a clown.*
chǫŭgh (chŭf), *a bird.*
ɛoin, *metal stamped.*
ɛoiḡnǝ, *a corner.*
ɛōlǝ, *a kind of cabbage.*
ɛōạl, *carbon.*
fīnd, *to discover.*
fīnǝd, *did fine; mulcted.*
prĭnts, *calicoes.*
prĭnçǝ, *a king's son.*

ẉrēạk, *to revenge.*
rēek, *vapor.* [*dead.*
bịēr, *a carriage for the*
bēer, *fermented liquor.*
rĕst, *quietness; ease.*
ẉrĕst, *to turn; to twist.*
rĭng, *a circle.*
ẉrĭng, *to twist.*
rōtǝ, *repetition.*
ẉrōtǝ, *did write.*
strāịt, *a narrow channel.*
strāịgḥt, *not crooked.*
wāvǝ, *an undulation.*
wāịvǝ, *to refuse.*

Lesson 68.

bōle, *the body of a tree.*
bōwl, *a vessel.*
bōll, *a pod.*
nōse, *part of the face.*
knōws, *does know.*
mōte, *a particle.*
mōat, *a ditch.*
tōled, *allured.*
tōld, *did tell.*
tōlled, *did toll.*
rein, *part of a bridle.*
rāin, *falling water.*
reign, *to rule.*

hist, *hush!*
hissed, *did hiss.*
paws, *the feet of beasts.*
pause, *a stop.*
faun, *a sylvan god.*
fawn, *a young deer.*
prīde, *vanity.*
prīed, *did pry.*
wāin, *a wagon.*
wāne, *to decrease.*
sēe, *to behold.*
sēa, *a body of water.*
sï, *a term in music.*

Lesson 69.

a flōat'	pōst pōne'	dï lūte'	de mūre'
be lōw'	pro rōgue'	a new'	de plūme'
be mōan'	dis eōurse'	dis ūse'	re erupt'
be stōw'	de pōrt'	en sūe'	re eluse'
de plōre'	re mōte'	im būe'	re fūte'
a brĕast'	at tĕmpt'	a brĭdge'	e elĭpse'
a hĕad'	dis trĕss'	dis mĭss'	e vĭnce'
be frĭĕnd'	eon nĕet'	a mĭdst'	ex tĭnet'
be hĕad'	bur lĕsque'	be twĭxt'	for gĭve'
in flĕet'	de flĕet'	be wĭtch'	in flĭet'

Lesson 70.

Long Sounds of Vowels.

aṳ stēre̸'	de ꞔrēa̸se̸'	ap pēa̸l'	dis ꞔrēet'
be quēa̸th'	in ꞔrēa̸se̸'	ap pēa̸r'	en trēa̸t'
re vēre̸'	de mēa̸n'	ap pēa̸se̸'	ex trēme̸'
be sēech'	fu ṣēe'	ar rēa̸r'	ḡran dēe'
bo hēa̸'	re pēa̸l'	blas phēme̸'	im pēa̸ch'
a liǥht'	de serībe̸'	aꞔ quīre̸'	dis ǥuīṣe̸'
a w̸ry'	de spīṣe̸'	at trīte̸'	es quīre̸'
be ǥuīle̸'	pre serībe̸'	as sīǥn'	iḡ nīte̸'
be liē̸'	de ꞔlīne̸'	de mīṣe̸'	in quīre̸'
de prīve̸'	re quīte̸'	ꞔom prīṣe̸'	ma līǥn'

Lesson 71.

Words accented on the Penult.

a mĕnd'ed	ꞔon tĕnt'ed	dĭ lĕm'ma̸
an ġĕl'iꞔ	re flĕꞔt'ĭve̸	dis tĕm'per
ap pĕn'dix	de ꞔrĕp'it	do mĕs'tiꞔ
as sĕm'bly	de fĕnd'ant	em bĕl'lish
as sĕss'ment	de mĕr'it	em bĕz'zle̸
pa rĕnt'al	re frĕsh'ing	re dŭn'dant
po ĕt'iꞔ	re plĕn'ish	a sŭn'der
pre ṣĕnt'ed	re ṣĕnt'ment	ꞔon ꞔŭr'rent
pu trĕs'çent	re splĕn'dent	ef fŭl'ġent
pre vĕnt'ĭve̸	sur rĕn'der	en ꞔŭm'ber

Lesson 72.

Trisyllables with the short Sounds of the Vowels.

ae quĭt′tal	de lĭv′er	in sĭp′id
be nĭg̃′nant	dĭ mĭn′ish	in trĭn′sie
be wĭl′der	eon sĭst′ent	ma lĭg̃′nant
eom mĭt′ment	eon tĭn′g̃ent	pa çĭf′ie
eon sĭd′er	e nĭg̃′mà	pro hĭb′it
a bŏl′ish	ear bŏn′ie	em bŏd′y
ab hŏr′rent	eo lŏs′sus	har mŏn′ie
ae eŏm′plish	de mŏl′ish	im pŏs′tor
ad mŏn′ish	a pŏs′tāt̸	la eŏn′ie
al lŏt′ment	des pŏt′ie	ma sŏn′ie

Lesson 73.

härt, *the male deer.*
h̸eärt, *the seat of life.*
hē̸ar, *to perceive by the ear.*
hēr̸, *in this place.*
hē̸ard, *did hear.*
hĕrd, *a drove.*
hī̸, *to hasten.*
hīg̸h, *lofty.*
hĭm, *objective case of he.*
hy̆mṉ, *a song of praise.*
hōl̸, *an opening.*
ẉhōl̸, *all; entire.*

h̸our, *sixty minutes.*
our, *belonging to us.*
ĭn, *within.*
ĭnn, *a hotel.*
kēy̸, *a fastener.*
quay (kē), *a wharf.*
rḥ̸ym̸, *poetry.*
rīm̸, *white frost.*
k̸nŏt, *a fastening of cord.*
nŏt, *negation.*
k̸nōẉ, *to understand.*
nō, *not so.*

Lesson 74.

The Vowel in the last Syllable silent.

bā'eøn	swēet'øn	dăm'şøn	bĭt'tøn
tō'køn	trēạ'şøn	făt'tøn	drĭv'øn
brā'zøn	wēạk'øn	flăx'øn	kĭt'tøn
hă'vøn	wēạ'şøl	ḡlăd'døn	prĭş'øn
hā'zøl	høĭghţ'øn	hăp'pøn	quĭck'øn
māị̆d'øn	lĭghţ'øn	măd'døn	rĭş'øn
mā'søn	lĭk'øn	răv'øl	smĭt'tøn
rā'vøn	rīp'øn	săd'døn	stĭff'øn
shāk'øn	tīghţ'øn	rĕd'døn	swĭv'øl
wēạ'zøn	wĭd'øn	frĕsh'øn	ẉrĭt'tøn
tāk'øn	brō'køn	ō'pøn	făsţ'øn
wāk'øn	ₑlō'vøn	lĕạv'øn	ḡlĭs'ţøn
spōk'øn	frōz'øn	lĕngth'øn	drŭn̠k'øn
dēạ'eøn	ḡōld'øn	rĕck'øn	mŭt'tøn

Lesson 75.

The Vowel in the last Syllable not silent.

ₑrāẏ'on	ăsp'en	tăl'on	ḡlū'ten
dē'mon	ₑăb'in	wăḡ'on	çĭt'ron
çī'on	drăḡ'on	sŭd'den	kĭţch'en
sī'phon	flăḡ'on	fēl'on	mĭt'ten
ₑō'lon	lĭn'den	lĕm'on	pĭs'ton
ō'men	ḡrăv'el	mĕl'on	hĕr'on
băr'rel	bĕv'el	chăn'nel	flăn'nel
pär'çel	plăt'en	chĭck'en	slŏv'en

Lesson 76.

Dissyllables with the long Sounds of the Vowels.

ā'g̅ū̵	fā'mŏŭs	eā̵'tiff	çī'pher
eā'lyx	fā̵l'ūr̵	frā'eas	hīg̅h'land
e̵h̵ā'os	fā̵th'fu̵l	g̅āt̵'-wāy̵	mō'hâ̵r
dā̵'ly	frā̵l'ty	nām̵'sāk̵	ōa̵k'um
dā̵'sy	g̅ām̵'ster	strā'tum	pōu̵l'tiç̵
bēa̵'dl̵	nēa̵t'ly	mēa̵'sl̵s̵	trēa̵'el̵
bēa̵'ver	e̵lēa̵r'anç̵	pē̵'pl̵	trēa̵'tīs̵
drēa̵r'y	e̵rē'denç̵	lē'g̅i̵ŏn	trēa̵t'ment
ēa̵'g̅er	flēe'çy	rē'g̅i̵ŏn	twēe'zers̵
mēa̵n'ness	g̅rēed'y	stēe'pl̵	wēa̵'ry

Lesson 77.

Words ending with *ow*, the last Letter being silent.

ăr'rō̵	săl'lō̵	fĕl'lō̵	wĭn'dō̵
hăr'rō̵	tăl'lō̵	mĕl'lō̵	wĭn'nō̵
năr'rō̵	shăl'lō̵	făl'lō̵	wĭd'ō̵
măr'rō̵	shăd'ō̵	mĕa̵d'ō̵	bŏr'rō̵
spăr'rō̵	ĕl'bō̵	bĭl'lō̵	mŏr'rō̵

Words containing *ei* or *ie*, promiscuously arranged.

g̅ri̵ēv̵	re tri̵ēv̵'	be si̵ēg̵̅	de çei̵v'er
thi̵ēv̵	ag̅ g̅ri̵ēv̵'	bre vi̵ēr'	de çei̵t'fu̵l
çei̵l̵d	a pi̵ēç̵'	de çei̵v̵'	dis sēi̵'zin
pi̵ēç̵d	e̵on çei̵t'	re li̵ēf'	a chi̵ēv'ing
shei̵k	be li̵ēv̵'	re li̵ēv̵'	re çei̵v'er

Lesson 78.

aught, *any thing.*
ôught, *should.*
wry, *crooked.*
rye, *a kind of grain.*
lead, *a metal.*
led, *did lead.*
read, *perused.*
red, *a color.*
read, *to peruse.*
reed, *a plant.*
all, *the whole.*
awl, *a sharp instrument.*

ōar, *for rowing.*
ōre, *unrefined metal.*
o'er, *over.*
ōw'er, *one who owes.*
ădds, *joins to.*
ădz, *a joiner's tool.*
āle, *a liquor.*
āil, *to feel pain.*
āte, *did eat.*
eight, *twice four.*
ànt, *an insect.*
äunt, *a relation.*

Lesson 79.

bald, *without hair.*
baẅlẹd, *cried out.*
băd, *ill; vicious.*
bădẹ, *past tense of bid.*
bäïzẹ, *a kind of cloth.*
bāỵş, *plural of bay.*
bẹâr, *an animal.*
bârẹ, *naked.*
bāỵ, *part of the ocean.*
beỵ, *a Turkish officer.*
bē, *to exist.*
bēe, *an insect.*

âïr, *the atmosphere.*
êrẹ, *before.*
ê'ẹr, *ever.*
ḥêïr, *one who inherits.*
āïşlẹ, *walk in a church.*
īşlẹ, *an island.*
Ī 'll, *I will.*
çērẹ, *to cover with wax.*
sēẹr, *to burn; dry.*
sēer, *a prophet.*
ball, *a round body.*
baẅl, *to cry out.*

Lesson 80.

gāỵ'ter
elĕv'er
pāỵnt'er
wāỵ'ward
dī'ġest
liġḥt'ning
pōr'traỵt
nŏv'ïçẹ
Tūẹş'dạy
eli'matẹ
ẅrïst'let

plănt'ạin
dăs'tard
seăb'bard
seăf'fold
shăm'blẹş
trăn'seript
nĕsṭ'ling
mĕn'açẹ
pĕn'ançẹ
shĕp'ḥerd
ẅhōlẹ'sŏmẹ

shrïv'ẹl
jŏs'ṭlẹ
bŭt'tọn
pïe'nïe
ġrŭm'blẹ
hŭs'ṭlẹ
mŭr'rạin
rŭm'blẹ
trọŭb'lẹ
är'ḡūẹ
pïn'çerş

jäụn'dïçẹ
sī'lex
màs'tiff
sär'eaşm
tär'nish
tär'tar
ha răngụẹ'
re lăpsẹ'
pro fĕss'
re vĕnġẹ'
flïġḥt'ỹ

Lesson 81.

DICTATION EXERCISES.

To essay the task, requires courage. The discourse was an able essay. An agent will assay the ore, and forward a receipt. Contemn a mean act; but do not always condemn the actor. They were to seize the fort, and cease firing. They affect great grief; but do not effect their purpose. Do you dissent from my opinion? The hill was difficult of descent. A decent regard for others' ills is human. They advise the young to take the advice of the old. The enemy will invade the rich province. They were strongly inveighed against.

Lesson 82.

ĕd'ū eāte̸	ĕm'er y	mĕth'od ĭst
ĕb'on y	ĕx'o dŭs	pĕn'i tent
ĕf'fi ġy	fĕl'o ný	sĕn'ti nel
ĕl'e phant	ġĕn'e sĭs	fĕl'lōẃ shĭp
ĕm'bas sy	fĕd'er al	rĕṣ'i dent
ăd'mi ral	eăn'ni bal	mȳr'i ad
ăġ'o ny	făe'to ry	slĭp'per y
ăl'i ment	ḡăl'ler y	mĭn'ū ĕnd
ăl'eo hŏl	măn'ū al	tȳr'an ny
ăm'nes ty	păr'a sŏl	sȳm'pho ny

Lesson 83.

mŭl′bĕr ry	ĕul′ti vātє́	ăm′ū let
mŭs′єu lar	jŭs′ti fȳ	ăn′çes try
pŭn′ish ment	mŭl′ti plȳ	Єăl′va ry
sŭb′se quent	mŭl′ti tūdє́	єăv′al ry
sŭp′pli єant	sŭb′sti tūtє́	măr′i ḡōld
ăm′pli fȳ	єăm′o mīlє́	băt′ter y
ḡrăt′i fȳ	păn′to mīmє́	єăn′o py
păç′i fȳ	răd′i єal	chăr′i ty
răr′e fȳ	păt′ron īzє́	chăs′ti ty
săn̠є′ti fȳ	săt′el lītє́	măj′es ty

Lesson 84.

bā͟il, *surety.*	bōld, *brave.*
bālє́, *a pack of goods.*	bōẃlє́d, *did bowl.*
bā͟it, *a lure.*	bōúrn, *a limit.*
bātє́, *to lessen.*	bōrnє́, *carried.*
bāsє́, *low; vile.*	bōẃ, *a weapon.*
bāss, *a part in music.*	beau (bō), *a man of dress.*
bēє́ch, *the shore.*	brєāk, *to sever by force.*
bēech, *a kind of tree.*	brākє́, *a thicket.*
bēє́t, *to strike.*	bru͟i͟sє́, *to crush.*
bēet, *a vegetable.*	brews̠ (bru͟z), *does brew.*
bĭn, *a box.*	bȳ, *near.*
been (bĭn), *existed.*	búȳ, *to purchase.*

Lesson 85.

bẽrth, *a sleeping-place.*
bĩrth, *coming into life.*
brăĭd, *to weave.*
brāyẹd, *did bray.*
brẹ́ach, *a gap.*
brēech, *the hinder part.*
brŏ́ach, *a spit; to pierce.*
brōoch, *an ornament.*
bŭt, *except.*
bŭtt, *a cask; a mark.*
ẹall, *to name.*
ẹaụl, *a kind of net-work.*

ẹàst, *to throw.*
ẹàstẹ, *an order or class.*
çēdẹ, *to yield.*
sēed, *to sow; to scatter.*
ẹōạrsẹ, *not fine.*
ẹōụrsẹ, *way; career.*
dăm, *mother of beasts.*
dămṇ, *to condemn.*
ẹānẹ, *a reed; a staff.*
Ɛ̄aĭn, *a man's name.*
çēĭl, *to line the top of.*
sēạl, *a sea animal.*

Lesson 86.

DICTATION EXERCISES.

The ensign would not sign the paper. His design was known. He maligned his rival, and suffered condign punishment. A benign face. He was arraigned after the campaign. He deigned not to feign surprise. Squirrels gnaw the bark. He affirmed it with phlegm. The knight carried a knapsack. He had a knack for rhymes. She knew how to knead the dough. They cut the knot with a knife. The curfew tolls the knell of parting day. The knave had hard knuckles, but little knowledge.

Lesson 87.

Sounds of O and U.

eŏn'dor	sŏl'id	ŏr'angǥ	spŏn'dēe
dŏe'trĭnǥ	lŏz'engǥ	ŏs'trich	tŏe'sin
eŏs'tĭvǥ	ŏf'fal	pŏmp'ǿŭs	jŏck'ǿy
fŏs'sil	ŏf'fĭçǥ	pŏn'tiff	mŏt'lǿy
frŏst'y	ŏl'ĭvǥ	prŏm'ĭsǥ	nŏs'trum
tŏn'nagǥ	nŏv'el	eŭm'brŏŭs	bŭck'lǥ
wŏn'der	bōot'y	eŭs'tard	bŭs'ţlǥ
wŏn'drŏŭs	movǥ'ment	flǿŭr'ish	dŭd'gǥŏn
wŏnt'ed	stŭe'eo	hŭn'dred	dŭn'gǥŏn
wŏr'rў	bŭz'zard	hŭṣ'band	lŭnch'ǿŏn

Lesson 88.

Short Sounds of Vowels.

dǿŭb'lǥ	bĕd'stĕạd	ĕb'on	fĕnd'er
ķnŭck'lǥ	chĕr'ub	ĕph'od	hĕạv'y
nǿŭr'ish	eres'çent	ĕs'sençǥ	hĕïf'er
sǿŭth'ern	erĕv'ĭçǥ	ĕth'ies	jĕạl'ǿŭs
frŭs'trātǥ	dĕx'trŏŭs	fçạth'er	jĕl'ly
rĕp'tĭlǥ	stĕr'ĭlǥ	brĭm'stōnǥ	ăb'bess
rĕf'ūsǥ	vĕs'tĭgǥ	die'tātǥ	ăd'junet
sĕn'tençǥ	wĕd'lŏck	frĭġ'atǥ	dăġ'ġer
skĕp'tie	Wĕđnǥṣ'dạў	pĭl'lagǥ	brăm'blǥ
spĕck'lǥ	zĕạl'ǿŭs	trĭb'ūtǥ	eăl'lǿŭs

Lesson 89.

çĕll, *a small room.*
sĕll, *to barter away.*
çĕnt, *a small coin.*
sĕnt, *did send.*
sçĕnt, *odor; smell.*
chāsĕd, *did chase.*
chāstĕ, *pure.* [*tence.*
claṷsĕ, *part of a sen-*
claẉs̱, *the nails of a beast.*
côrd, *a small rope.*
chôrd, *musical tones in harmony.*
côtĕ, *a pen; a fold.*
côạt, *an outer garment.*

eärt, *a vehicle.*
eärtĕ, *a bill of fare.*
dĕạr, *costly; beloved.*
dēer, *an animal.*
dūĕ, *owing; fit.*
dew (dū), *moisture con-densed.*
dōĕ, *the female deer.*
dōụgh, *unbaked paste.*
drăm, *a glass of spirits.*
drăchm, *a small weight.*
fānĕ, *a temple.*
fạịn, *gladly.*
feịgn, *to pretend.*

Lesson 90.

be spēạk′
nan kēen′
im plēạd′
con çēạl′
con ġēạl′

ab sŏlvĕ″
de vŏlvĕ″
dis̱ s̱ŏlvĕ″
re s̱ŏlvĕ″
re spŏnd′

ad jŭḏġĕ″
be ġrŭḏġĕ″
sub dŭet′
be nŭmḃ′
con vŭlsĕ″

in dŭlġĕ″
re pŭlsĕ″
sue eŭmḃ′
af frŏnt′
a mòng′

re frạịn′
re mạịn′
re strạịn′
re tạịn′
re tạịl′

re prĭnt′
re strĭet′
re s̱ĭst′
sub mĭt′
dis tĭṉet′

re prōạch′
en erōạch′
pa trōl′
pa rōlĕ″
be fōrĕ″

re tākĕ″
re trāçĕ″
re pāy′
de lāy′
al lāy′

Lesson 91.

dŭst, *powdered earth.*
dȯst, *second person of do.*
ẽȧrn, *to gain by labor.*
ûrn, *a kind of vase.*
ẽrn, *the sea-eagle.*
dĭe̸, *to expire.*
dȳe̸, *to color.*
drau̸ght (drȧft), *drawing.*
drȧft, *a bill of exchange.*
dŭn, *a dark color.*
dȯne̸, *performed.*
fāte̸, *destiny.*
fẹte̸, *a festival.*

dāy̸, *twenty-four hours.*
dey̸, *a Turkish title.*
ewe (yṳ), *a female sheep.*
yø̤ṳ, *the person spoken to.*
yew (yṳ), *a kind of tree.*
e̸ȳe̸, *the organ of sight.*
Ī, *myself.*
äÿ, *yes.*
äÿe̸, *an affirmative vote.*
flēe, *to run away.*
flēa̸, *an insect.*
flew (flū), *did fly.*
flūe̸, *a passage for smoke.*

Lesson 92.

ăġ'ĭle̸	hăck'ne̸y	păs'sĭve̸	bĭs'eu̸it
ăl'ōe̸ṣ	ḳnăp'săck	prăe'tĭçe̸	fĭl'bert
dăe'tyl	lăd'der	răb'id	ĭm'aġe̸
făsh'ĭȯn	lăt'tĭçe̸	răp'id	ĭm'pulse̸
ġăl'le̸y	lăn'çet	tăe'ties	mĭl'dew
bĭt'tern	erŷs'tal	erĭm'ṣȯn	kĭd'ne̸y
brĭsk'et	dĭs'tançe̸	ġrĭd'dle̸	lĭn'tel
çĭs'tern	dĭs'taff	live̸'lŏng	lĭq'uid
chĭm'ne̸y	dwĭn'dle̸	ġŷp'sy	lĭq'u̸ȯr
chĭṣ'e̸l	pĭck'le̸	hĭth'er	rĭd'dançe̸

Lesson 93.

slŭi̵'çy	bŏl'ster	çẽr'tạin	drĭz'zl₡
jŭi̵'çy	€ōu̵rt'shĭp	sûr'ly	tĭck'l₡
stew'ard	frō'ward	sûr'ġ₡òn	twĭn̲k'l₡
jew'el	€ō'€ōạ	ẽạr'nest	thĭm'bl₡
n₡ū'tral	nōs₡'ġāy̵	jø̵ûr'nal	vĭl'lạin
€ôr'ner	ġôr'ġon	ạṳ'dit	sō'dȧ
€ôr'sâi̵r	lôrd'shĭp	€ạṳs'ti€	sō'fȧ
€ôrs₡'let	môr'bid	aṵk'ward	sō'ber
fôr'f₡it	môrṱ'ġaġ₡	ġaṳd'y	stō'i€
ġôr'ġ₡ø̵ŭs	môr'sel	laṵ'rel	tō'paz

Lesson 94.

DICTATION EXERCISES.

The awl is used by all shoe-makers. He
said that he would do aught that he ought to
do. The man who stole the bale of goods gave
bail. The Bey rode a bay horse around the
bay. Deer break through the brake and
brush. He had just lain down in the narrow
lane. The horse with the long mane ran
through the main street of a town in Maine.
Which of the pair of fine pears will you pare
for the child? The joiner's plane will smooth
the plain door. You can rein your horse, if it
should rain. The kings reign wisely.

Lesson 95.

băl'us trādé	făb'ri eāté	běv'er agé
ăl'ka lĭ	ḡăl'ax y	chěr'ṵ bĭm
ăl'ka lĭné	măs'to don	děm'o erăt
ăp'o ḡee	măck'er el	děn'ĭ zén
ăl'i quot	măr'i ner	děn'si ty
ăs'ter ĭsk	păr'a ḡrăph	ěx'or çĭst
ăz'i mŭth	păr'al lăx	ěd'i fȳ
băch'e lor	păr'a ḡŏn	ěm'a nāté
eăl'a băsh	păr'a pět	ěm'pha sīzé
eăl'a mŭs	păr'a phrāṣé	ěp'i eūré

Lesson 96.

fīr, *a kind of tree.*
fûr, *soft hair.*
fāịnt, *weak; languid.*
feịnt, *a pretense.*
fâịr, *clear; handsome.*
fâré, *food; cost of passage.*
feet, *plural of foot.*
feạt, *an exploit.*
flōé, *a large piece of ice.*
flōẃ, *a current.*
flour, *ground wheat.*
flow'er, *a blossom.*

fōrt, *a stronghold.*
fōrté, *one's strong point.*
fōrth, *forward.*
fōṵrth, *the next after third.*
frāẏṣ, *quarrels.*
phrāṣé, *part of a sentence.*
fōré, *toward the front.*
fōṵr, *twice two.*
foul, *impure.*
fowl, *a bird.*
freezé, *to become ice.*
frịezé, *a kind of cloth.*

Lesson 97.

ĕx'pe dītĕ	pĕd'i ment	eŭr'ren çy
hĕl'le bōrĕ	pĕl'i ean	fŭl'sŏmĕ ly
pĕr'i ḡee	pĕt'ū lant	nŭl'li ty
rĕḡ'i çīdĕ	rĕe'om pĕnsĕ	sŭb'si dy
rĕe'on dītĕ	sphĕr'ie al	sŭb'ter fūḡĕ
fīf'tĭ eth	sўn'o nўm	eŏn'ju ḡātĕ
mĭr'a ĕlĕ	tўr'an nīzĕ	eŏn'tro vērt
nĭm'blĕ ness	wĭtch'er y	eŏn'se erātĕ
rĭḡ'or ŏŭs	wĭl'der ness	eŏr'o net
rĭṣ'i blĕ	whĭm'ṣi eal	dŏm'i nant

Lesson 98.

är'bi trātĕ	härd'i hŏŏd	fôr'mu là
är'ma ment	här'le qŭĭn	ḡôr'mand īzĕ
är'mis tĭçĕ	eär'ni val	ôr'der ly
är'eĥi tĕet	eär'bon atĕ	ôr'di nal
ärch'er y	ḡär'dĕn er	ôr'di natĕ
bär'ba rĭṣm	ḡär'ni tūrĕ	ôr'phan aḡĕ
dĕç'i mal	mĕt'a phor	erĭt'i çĭṣm
dĕs'pot ĭṣm	ĕd'it or	çўl'in der
ĕm'pha sis	sĕn'a tor	mўs'ter y
ĕp'i tăph	sĕr'a phĭm	mўs'ti fў
lĕth'ar ḡy	spĕç'i men	phўṣ'ie al
pĕn'ta tĕūeĥ	spĕe'ū lātĕ	tўp'i fў

Sp. 5.

Lesson 99.

Short and long Sounds of the Vowels.

bŭt′ler	eŏm′mon	dĭṣ′mal	blĕm′ish
bŭck′ler	dŏḡ′må	dĭs′trıet	elĕm′ent
eŭd′ġel	dŏl′phin	mĭm′ie	chĕr′ry
jŭḋġ′ment	hŏs′tĭlę	mĭs′sĭvę	erĕd′it
snŭff′erṣ	mŏd′ern	sўn′od	ĕm′berṣ
bŏnd′aġę	eŏn′vent	elī′măx	āịd′ançę
eŏt′taġę	sŏph′ist	fī′brøŭs	bāịl′iff
fŏr′aġę	sŏr′rel	hȳ′brid	bāsę′ment
hŏs′taġę	stŏp′plę	hȳ′men	brāçę′let
prŏs′trātę	tŏd′dy	hȳ′phen	brāvę′ly

Lesson 100.

fûrṣ, *skins with soft hair.*
fûrzé, *a prickly shrub.*
ḡȧg̣é, *to pledge.*
ḡȧu̧g̣é, *to measure.*
ḡȧté, *door; entrance.*
ḡȧi̧t, *manner of walking.*
ḡïlt, *adorned with gold.*
g̣u̧ïlt, *crime.*
ḡrȩ́at, *large; vast.*
ḡrȧté, *a range of bars.*
ḡrȩ́aṣé, *soft fat.*
Ḡrēȩçé, *a country.*

ḡrō̧an, *a deep sigh.*
ḡrōẏn, *increased.*
ḡa̧ll, *bile.*
Ḡau̧l, *old name of France.*
ḡïld, *to overlay with gold.*
g̣u̧ïld, *a corporation.*
ḡlōzé, *to smooth over.*
ḡlōẏṣ, *shines.*
g̣u̧ést, *a visitor.*
g̣u̧éssé́d, *did guess.*
hālé, *sound; healthy.*
hȧi̧l, *frozen rain.*

Lesson 101.

a lẽrt′	ex pẽrt′	sub vẽrt′	re mo̧vé″
as sẽrt′	in ẽrt′	su pẽrb′	a do̧′
a vẽr′	in fẽr′	ab sûrd′	a lōōf′
a vẽrt′	in sẽrt′	re ȩûr′	bal lōōn′
ȩon çẽrn′	in vẽrt′	de mûr′	buf fōōn′
per vẽrt′	pre fẽr′	dis tûrb′	hal lōō′
a vȧi̧l′	re ȩlȧi̧m′	dis plāẏ′	be fa̧ll′
a wȧi̧t′	ab stȧi̧n′	en tȧi̧l′	re ȩall′
de ȩāẏ′	ae quȧi̧nt′	ob tȧi̧n′	en thra̧ll′
de ȩlȧi̧m′	af frāẏ′	ȩon tȧi̧n′	re ṣort′
de frāẏ′	as suȧg̣é′	per suȧdé′	as sôrt′
pre vȧi̧l′	block ādé″	a brǫad′	be sôu̧g̣ẖt′

Lesson 102.

ăl'phȧ	păd'lŏck	ăd'dlḗ	hŏn'ḗy
ăn'ĭsḗ	plăç'id	băr'rack	ȼŏm'fŏrt
brăck'et	Săb'bath	măn'datḗ	mŏth'er
dăm'ask	săf'fron	măn'ly	ŏth'er
măd'der	stăḡ'nant	stăḡ'nātḗ	smŏth'er
ȼlŏṣ'et	ȼŏn'trītḗ	chĕr'ish	vĕs'tal
ȼŏm'ment	ŏȼ'tavḗ	dĕn'tist	lĕḡ'atḗ
ȼŏn̄'ȼŏ𝑢rsḗ	vŏl'ūmḗ	frĕsh'et	mĕm'brānḗ
ȼŏn'text	bŏn'fīrḗ	rĕl'ish	mĕs'saḡḗ
ȼŏn'vex	ȼŏn̄'q𝑢er	rĕm'nant	rĕs'ȼūḗ

Lesson 103.

flout	a frĕsh'	fīr'kin	ā'er ātḗ
mĕánt	ȼon tĕm𝑢'	sērv'īlḗ	lā'i ty
𝑤rĕn	ȼon tĕmpt'	skīr'mish	dē'vi ǿus
quĭck	ȼom mȧnd'	stēr'ling	rē'al īzḗ
sŏlvḗ	ȼom mĕnȼḗ'	sûr'fḗĭt	rē'qui em
𝑤rŏng	ȼom mĕnd'	ûr'ḡent	ȼō'ḡen çy
quĭnȼḗ	ȼom păȼt'	fûr'lŏ𝑢ḡh	nō'ti fȳ
shrĭmp	ȼom plāịnt'	jăṣ'mĭnḗ	pō'ten çy
ȼaụṣḗ	es trāy'	lăck'ḗy	ō'ri ōlḗ
ḡaụ́zḗ	ap prŏách'	lăṭch'et	ō'ri ent
quoin	ȼor rōdḗ'	măt'in	jō'vi al
squạ𝑤	ȼur tāịl'	seăt'ter	vō'ta ry
ȼrŏss	re pūtḗ'	săv'aḡḗ	zō'di ȧe

Lesson 104.

DICTATION EXERCISES.

I accept all your presents except the last.
His joy was in excess, at the news of his access
to fortune. Though your terms exceed my ex-
pectations, I must accede to them. The best
cosmetic is air and exercise. He pretended to
exorcise evil spirits. Both assent to go up
the ascent. He was indicted for inditing a
false letter. Champagne is made in France.
The soldiers crossed the champaign. The law
will levy a tax to build a levee. The levee
was held at the mayor's residence. The senior
brother was addressed as seignior.

Lesson 105.

çẽr'ti fȳ	fôr'ti fȳ	eŏḡ'ni zançe
fẽr'ti lize	fôr'ti tūde	eŏn'ju ḡal
hẽrb'al ĭst	fôrt'ū nate	ḡlŏb'ū lar
sẽrv'i tūde	ôr'di nançe	ŏr'i ḡĭn
tẽr'mi nāte	ôr'ḡan ĭşm	hŏm'i ly
fẽr'ven çy	är'bi ter	ăf'flu ent
mẽr'eu ry	är'ter y	băl'us ter
nûrs'er y	här'mo ny	băr'ri er
pẽr'fi dy	lär'çe ny	băr'ris ter
pẽr'ju ry	här'mo nīze	eăr'ri on

Lesson 106.

Words accented on the first Syllable.

elĕr'ie al	fĕs'ti val	lī'bra ry
ĕl'e ġy	ĕth'ie al	likę'li hŏod
ĕm'i ġrant	hĕr'ald ry	mī'ero eŏṣm
ĕm'per or	hĕr'e tie	mī'ero seōpę
ĕp'i ġrăm	hĕr'o ĭṣm	nī'tro ġen
pā'pa çy	dī'a leet	pĕd'ant ry
flā'ġran çy	dī'a ġrăm	pĕd'es tal
frā'ġran çy	dī'a ry	mĕd'i çinę
rā'di ançę	fĭn'er y	lĕx'i eon
slā'ver y	ī'vo ry	sĕd'ū lǿŭs
mā̤ı̨n'te nançę	plī'a blę	quĕr'u̜ lǿŭs

Lesson 107.

Monosyllables representing different Sounds.

strā̤y̨	slēet	strīkę	trōpę	eûrsę
āeḩę	flēeçę	trītę	ġrōpę	hēa̤rsę
bāthę	stēer	splıçę	brōkę	pûrġę
lāthę	spēech	strīpę	strōkę	seǿûrġę
plā̤ı̨nt	sphērę	tīthę	elōa̤k	vērġę
brā̤ı̨n	fı̤ēf	yı̤ēld	erŏck	squēa̤l
slāvę	fı̤ēld	fı̤ērçę	blŏck	lēa̤ġuę
quākę	thı̤ef	pı̤ērçę	flŏck	plēa̤d
stāvę	fı̤ēnd	tı̤ērçę	shŏck	squēa̤k
plāġuę	shrı̤ēk	nı̤ēçę	mŏck	hēa̤th

Lesson 108.

Synthetic Exercises.

Make Sentences containing the following Words.

bough, *a branch of a tree.*
bow, *to bend.*
brute, *a beast.*
bruit, *to noise abroad.*
çite, *to summon.*
sīte, *a situation.*
sīght, *the sense of seeing.*
ҫlimb, *to ascend.*
ҫlime, *climate; region.*
ҫōre, *the inner part.*
ҫōrps, *a body of soldiers.*
ҫreek, *a narrow inlet.*
ҫreak, *a grating noise.*

grīeves, *laments.* [*legs.*
grēaves, *armor for the*
hew (hū), *to cut; to chop.*
hūe, *a color; dye.*
Hūgh, *a man's name.*
kĭll, *to deprive of life.*
kĭln, *a large oven.*
lēaf, *of a tree or book.*
līef, *willingly; gladly.*
māze, *an intricate place.*
māize, *Indian corn.*
mēan, *low; middle point.*
mĭen, *air; manner.*

Lesson 109.

Miscellaneous Sounds.

bụl′let	ҫoͦop′er	nôr′mal	pre çise′
bụll′y	woͦol′en	ôr′phan	pre ṣide′
bụll′ock	ҫooͦl′ly	tôr′por	pro serībe′
bụl′rush	sҫoun′drel	quạr′ter	ҫom mōde′
bụsh′el	bạl′sam	aҫ ҫlāim′	en grōss′
bụll′ion	squạd′ron	o pāque′	ҫon sūme′
ҫrụp′per	wạr′rant	sea lēne′	pre ṣume′
ҫụck′oͦo	quạd′rant	se çede′	be dew′

Lesson 110,

falsȩ	naught	pitch	bătch	ĕdġȩ
quạrt	sought	flitch	mătch	hĕdġȩ
swạrd	bought	stitch	hătch	lĕdġȩ
swạrm	bright	fitch	lătch	wĕdġȩ
thwạrt	plīght	hitch	pătch	flĕdġȩ

bĭlġȩ	bŭdġȩ	fŏssȩ	brĕadth	twĭnġȩ
brĭdġȩ	jŭdġȩ	thŏng	brĕạst	prĭnt
rĭdġȩ	drŭdġȩ	nŏtch	clĕạnsȩ	flĭng
hĭnġȩ	grŭdġȩ	blŏtch	frĭend	strĭng
ẹrĭnġȩ	plŭnġȩ	prŏmpt	knĕll	swĭft

Lesson 111.

hạll, *a large room.*
haul, *to drag by force.*
hāy, *dried grass.*
he̤y! *an exclamation.*
hârȩ, *an animal.*
hâịr, *of the head.*
hēạl, *to cure.*
hēel, *hinder part of the foot.*
hīrȩ, *wages.*
high'er, *more high.*
hoȩ, *a farming tool.*
hō! *an exclamation.*

hōop, *a ring; a band.*
whōop, *to make a noise.*
hīȩd, *made haste.*
hīdȩ, *to conceal.*
hōạrd, *to lay up.*
hōrdȩ, *a tribe.*
hōȩṣ, *plural of hoe.*
hōṣȩ, *stockings.*
jăm, *a conserve of fruit.*
jămb, *the side-piece of a door or fire-place.*
knēạd, *to work dough.*
nēed, *want.*

Lesson 112.

fāịth	thēmé	lĕngth	sŏr'rōw	sŏl'emṇ
serāpé	chīmé	läunch	dūr'ing	hīré'ling
strāngé	whĭlst	môrgué	gĭb'bet	trĕs'pass
grēet	smärt	plĕdgé	bŏd'kin	shĭl'ling
pērch	bădgé	gōurd	gōs'ling	măt'tock
chămp	dŏdgé	sçhĭst	lŏb'by	răm'pärt
drĕnch	brawl	flouncé	tăn'sy	trăn'quil
squēezé	dwarf	serēech	lŏck'et	eŭn'ning
grĭst	yawl	spăsm	văn'dal	hĕr'ring
shrĭnk	grånt	stärvé	ĕx'trà	drŭg'gist
eŏpsé	spŭnk	seălp	eŭt'lass	spŏn'sor

Lesson 113.

knīght, a title of honor.
nīght, time of darkness.
knāvé, a wicked person.
nāvé, hub of a wheel.
lōan, any thing lent.
lōné, solitary. [ance.
knăp, a small protuber-
năp, a short sleep.
lăe, a kind of gum.
lăck, to want; need.
lāịd, placed.
lādé, to load.

lēe, the sheltered side.
lĕa, a meadow; field.
lié, to deceive. [ashes.
lÿé, water passed through
lĭnks, parts of a chain.
lÿnx, an animal.
lŏeḥ, a lake.
lŏugh (lŏk), a lake.
lŏck, to fasten a door.
lăx, loose; vague.
lăcks, wants; needs.
lăes, plural of lac.

Lesson 114.

Words containing I consonant, sounded like Y consonant; as *alien*, pronounced āl'yen.

āl'ien	ȯn'iȯn	bat tăl'iȯn
sāv'iọr	bĭl'iọ̆us	pe ̄eūl'iar
păn'nier	brĭll'iant	re bĕll'iȯn
ūn'iȯn	fīl'ial	dis ūn'iȯn
sēn'iȯr	mĭll'iȯn	o pĭn'iȯn
jūn'iȯr	pĭll'iȯn	do mĭn'iȯn
g̃ăl'liard	pĭn'iȯn	̄eom mūn'iȯn
spăn'iel	trĭll'iȯn	mūt'ū al
văl'iant	̄eȯll'ier	punẹ tĭl'io
bĭll'iardş	pŏn'iard	punẹ tĭl'iọ̆us
bĭll'iȯn	rŭf'fian	ver mĭl'iȯn
Ĭn'dian	̄Çⱨrĭs'tian	aṉx̱ ĭl'ia rӯ

Lesson 115.

The following words, according to the analogy of the English language, should be spelled with the termination *er*, with the exception of the last word of each line.

çĕn'ter	mī'ter	spĕe'ter	sĕp'ul ̄eⱨⱦer
fī'ber	nī'ter	ō'̄eⱨⱦer	thē'a ter
lŭs'ter	sŏm'ber	maⱨ'g̃er	ma n̄ēū'ver
mĕⱥ'g̃er	sā'ber	ŭm'ber	̄eăl'i ber
mē'ter	s̄ēĕp'ter	ŏm'ber	ae ̄eoⱨ'ter
ā'erⱦ	nā'erⱦ	lū'erⱦ	mās'sa erⱦ

Lesson 116.

In the following words, *ng* is pronounced as if the *g* were doubled; as *anger*, pronounced ăng′ḡer.

ăn′ḡer	lăn′guŏr	jĭn′ḡlĕ	yŏŭn′ḡer
ăn′ḡlĕ	lăn′ḡuid	mĭn′ḡlĕ	ċŏn′ḡer
ăn′ḡry	măn′ḡlĕ	sĭn′ḡlĕ	bŭn′ḡler
ăn′ḡuish	măn′ḡo	tĭn′ḡlĕ	hŭn′ḡer
ċlăn′ḡor	săn′ḡuĭnĕ	dĭn′ḡlĕ	hŭn′ḡry
dăn′ḡlĕ	spăn′ḡlĕd	lŏn′ḡer	ẇrăn′ḡler
făn′ḡlĕd	spăn′ḡlĕ	lŏn′ḡest	fĭn′ḡer
jăn′ḡlĕ	tăn′ḡlĕ	strŏn′ḡer	lăn′ḡuish
băn′ḡlĕ	ẇrăn′ḡlĕ	bŭn′ḡlĕ	ŭn′ḡuent

Lesson 117.

In the following, S has the sound of *sh;* as *sure,* (pro. shure).

sure͢'ly	çĕn'sure͢	fĭs'sure͢	ĭs'su͢ ançe͢
sure͢'ness	prĕss'ūre͢	tŏn'sure͢	as sur'ançe͢
sure͢'ty	ĭs'su͢e͢	as sure͢'	in sur'ançe͢
su͢g̅'ar	tĭs'su͢e͢	in sure͢'	in sur'er

The following words are spelled, according to analogy, with the termination *se.*

ȼon dĕnse͢'	dis pĕnse͢'	im mĕnse͢'	pre tĕnse͢'
de fĕnse͢'	ex pĕnse͢'	of fĕnse͢'	sus pĕnse͢'
re çĕnse͢'	in çĕnse͢'	pre pĕnse͢'	lĭ'çense͢

Lesson 118.

lāne͢, *a narrow passage.*	māĭn, *chief.* [*a horse.*
lāĭn, *past participle of lie.*	māne͢, *hair on the neck of*
	māĭl, *armor.*
lăpse͢, *to fall.*	māle͢, *masculine.*
lăps, *plural of lap.*	märk, *a sign.* [*prisal.*
lea͢k, *to run out.*	märque͢, *letters of re-*
lēek, *a kind of onion.*	mēa͢d, *a drink.*
lō! *behold!*	mēed, *reward.*
lōw͢, *not high.*	mēet, *fit; proper.*
lōre͢, *learning.*	mēte͢, *to measure.*
lōw͢'er, *more low.*	mēa͢t, *food in general.*
māĭd, *a maiden.*	mīg͢ht, *strength; power.*
māde͢, *finished.*	mīte͢, *a small insect.*

Lesson 119.

mōdₑ, *way; manner.*
mōwₑd, *cut down.*
mūlₑ, *an animal.*
mewl (mūl), *to squall.*
mĭst, *fine rain.*
mĭssₑd, *did miss.*
mōrₑ, *a greater quantity.*
mōw′er, *one who mows.*
mūsₑ, *to meditate.*
mews (mūz), *an in-*
  closure.
nònₑ, *not one.*
nŭn, *a religious woman.*

nāy, *no.*
neĭgh, *to cry as a horse.*
nĭt, *egg of an insect.*
knĭt, *to unite.*
gnēĭss, *a kind of min-*
  eral.
nīçₑ, *delicate; fine.*
ōwₑ, *to be bound.*
ōh! *alas!*
ōdₑ, *a poem.*
ōwₑd, *indebted.*
one (wŭn), *a single thing.*
wòn, *gained.*

Lesson 120.

a măl′ğam ātₑ
as săs′sin ātₑ
ċa păç′i tātₑ
ċo ăğ′ū lātₑ
ċon ċat′e nātₑ
ċon făb′ū lātₑ
ċon ğrăt′ū lātₑ
ċon tăm′i nātₑ
de ċăp′i tātₑ
e jăċ′ū lātₑ
e lăb′o rātₑ

chēesₑ
dīrt
blḝak
ğō̧ad
slouch
ğŏnₑ
sċärf
nẽrvₑ
rāẙd
ğrāzₑ
stālₑ

e măn′çi pātₑ
e răd′i ċatₑ
e văċ′ū ātₑ
a băn′don ment
in făt′ū ātₑ
in văl′i dātₑ
be ăt′i fȳ
pro ċrăs′ti nātₑ
re tăl′i ātₑ
e văp′o rātₑ
pre văr′i ċātₑ

Lesson 121.

çīr'eus	ea păç'i ty	ăn'a ḡrăm
eûr'few	eom păr'i son	ăm'bĭ ent
eûr'tạin	eom păr'a tĭvé	ăl'li ḡāté
fẽr'tĭlé	eom păt'i blé	eăl'a mĭné
fẽr'vid	eon eăv'i ty	hăl'çў on
fûr'naçé	de elăr'a tĭvé	Jĕṣ'ū it
fûr'long	dī ăḡ'o nạl	pĕd'i ḡrēe
mẽr'māĭd	dī ăm'e ter	rĕḡ'is ter
nẽrv'ǿŭs	doḡ măt'ie al	rĕv'el ry
pûr'chasé	em băs'sa dor	skĕp'tie al
sûr'façé	de prăv'i ty	vĕr'i ly

Lesson 122.

In words like the following, *sier, zier, sure, zure, su, sion,* and *sia* are pronounced zhûr, zhụr, zhū, zhŭn, and zhả.

brā'ṣier	em brā'ṣuré	eăṣ'ū al ly
ḡlā'zier	e rāṣ'ūré	eăṣ'ū ist ry
ḡrā'zier	e vā'ṣiȯn	trĕạ̇ṣ'ūr er shĭp
rāṣ'ūré	in vā'ṣiȯn	ūṣ'ū al ly
sēĭz'ūré	per suā'ṣiȯn	plĕạ̇ṣ'ur a blé
hō'ṣier	ad hē'ṣiȯn	mĕạ̇ṣ'ūr a blé
ō'ṣier	eo hē'ṣiȯn	oe eā'ṣiȯn al
fū'ṣiȯn	am brō'ṣiả	pro vĭṣ'iȯn al
ăz'uré	dis elōṣ'ūré	u ṣū'rĭ ǿŭs
mĕạ̇ṣ'ūré	ex plō'ṣiȯn	dĭs eom pōṣ'uré
plĕạ̇ṣ'uré	eol lū'ṣiȯn	ĭn de çĭṣ'iȯn

Lesson 123.

Synthetic and Dictation Exercises.

brīd'al, *belonging to a bride.*

brī'dlḗ, *a check; a curb.*

lĕs'sŏn, *a task for recitation.*

lĕss'ḗn, *to make less.*

mĕt'al, *a substance.*

mĕt'tlḗ, *spirit.*

vīçḗ, *defect; fault.*

vīsḗ, *an instrument.*

wāı̆l, *to lament.*

wālḗ, *to mark with stripes.*

Filled with choler, he seized the youth by the collar. The priest filled the censer. He is a censor of the press. The ship took divers persons as divers for pearls. The plaintiff assumed a plaintive air. To lessen the number of exercises, will make an easier lesson.

Lesson 124.

serĭvḗ'ner	frĭv'o lḗŭs	frṳ ḡăl'i ty
slŭḡ'ḡard	ĭm'aḡḗ ry	ḡram măt'ie al
stŭb'born	ĭn'di ḡo	hī lăr'i ty
sŭb'urbṣ	ĭn'sti ḡātḗ	hu măn'i ty
sў̆mp'tom	lĭq'uĭ dātḗ	in hăb'it ant
mĕd'lḗy	pīl'ḡrim aḡḗ	ī răs'çi blḗ
pĕḁs'ant	fĭsh'er y	le ḡăl'i ty
phĕḁs'ant	hĭck'o ry	lo ℮ăl'i ty
pĕn'sĭvḗ	ĭn'ter est	lo quăç'i ty
prĕṣ'ençḗ	mĭt'ti mŭs	men dăç'i ty
rĕḁd'y	mĭn'strel sy	ra păç'i ty

Lesson 125.

Note.—These words are not exactly alike in sound, and should be carefully distinguished.

as sĭst'ançé, *help; relief.*
as sĭst'ants, *helpers.*
de vīṣ'er, *an inventor.*
dĭ vī'ṣor, *a term in Arith-metic.*
dĕf'er ençé, *respect.*
dĭf'fer ençé, *variation.*
in ġĕn'ū ǿŭs, *open; free.*
in ġēn'iǿŭs, *having skill.*

răb'bit, *an animal.*
răb'bet, *a term in car-pentry.*
lĭn'e a ment, *a feature.*
lĭn'i ment, *an ointment.*
prĭn'çi pal, *chief.*
prĭn'çi plé, *rule of action.*
lī'ar, *one who tells lies.*
lȳré, *a kind of harp.*

Lesson 126.

DICTATION EXERCISES ON THE ABOVE.

His assistants gave him great assistance. He was the deviser of the machine. Which is the larger, the divisor or the quotient? This difference being settled, he will pay due deference to your opinion. The ingenious mechanic was also an ingenuous man. Not a lineament could be recognized by his friends. Apply to the wound a healing liniment. The principal in the agreement was devoid of moral principle. Though a great liar, he could play upon the lyre. The rabbit was tame. The carpenter will rabbet the boards.

Lesson 127.

In words like the following, U should receive its proper consonant sound; as *nature*, pronounced nāt′yur̤.

nāt′ūr̨	sĭg̅′na tūr̨	ăg̅′ri ̨eŭlt ūr̨
̨erēạt′ūr̨	sĕp′ul tūr̨	lĕg̅′is lā tūr̨
f̅ēạt′ūr̨	fûr′ni tūr̨	är′e̦ḥi tĕet ūr̨
fūt′ūr̨	fôr′f̨ei̯t ūr̨	tĕm′per a tūr̨
̨eăpt′ūr̨	lĭg̅′a tūr̨	lit′er a tūr̨
răpt′ūr̨	ăp′er tūr̨	flō′ri ̨eŭlt ūr̨
tĕxt′ūr̨	quạd′ra tūr̨	jū′di ̨ea tūr̨
pĭet′ūr̨	ad vĕnt′ūr̨	hôr′ti ̨eŭlt ūr̨
serĭpt′ūr̨	̨eon jĕet′ūr̨	măn ū fą̆et′ūr̨

Lesson 128.

pāi̯l, *a wooden vessel.*
pāl̨, *not bright.*
p̨eâr, *a fruit.*
pâr̨, *to cut thin.*
pâi̯r, *a couple.*
rāz̨, *to pull down.*
rāi̯ṣ̨, *to lift up.*
rāy̧ṣ, *beams of light.*
pāi̯n, *uneasiness.*
pān̨, *a square of glass.*
pēel, *rind; skin.*
pę̄al, *a sound of bells.*
pōrt, *a harbor.*
Pōrt̨, *a Turkish court.*

Pau̧l, *a man's name.*
pạll, *a covering.*
pĭqu̧̨, *to give offense.*
pę̄ak, *the top.*
pēer, *a nobleman.*
pi̯ēr, *a wharf.*
quạrtz, *a kind of rock.*
quạrts, *measures.*
plāi̯n, *smooth.*
plān̨, *a surface; tool.*
quīr̨, *twenty-four sheets*
  of paper.
choir (kwīr), *a band of*
  singers.

Lesson 129.

X with the sound of *gz;* as *exact,* pronounced eḡz ăet'.

ex ăet'	ex ăet'ly	ex ăg̣'g̣er āt¢
ex ĭst'	ex ăm'ĭn¢	ex ăn'i māt¢
ex ŭlt'	ex ĕm'plar	ex ăs'per āt¢
ex hāl¢'	ex ēr'tion	ex ĕe'ū trĭx
ex haṵst'	ex hĭb'it	ex hĭl'a rāt¢
ex ērt'	ex ĭst'enç¢	ex ŏn'er āt¢
ex hôrt'	ex ĭst'ent	ex ĕm'pli fȳ
ex ūd¢'	ex ŏt'ie	ex ôr'bi tant
ex ērg̣ṵ¢'	ex haṵst'ĭv¢	ux ō'rĭ ¢ŭs

Lesson 130.

Ti has often the sound of *sh:* followed by *on*, it is pronounced shŭn.

nā'tion	çĕs sā'tion	dē vĭ ā'tion
pā'tient	eol lā'tion	dĕp re dā'tion
făe'tiøŭs	ere ā'tion	dĕs per ā'tion
frăe'tiøŭs	die tā'tion	lĭb er ā'tion
stā'tion	do nā'tion	mē dĭ ā'tion
lō'tion	du rā'tion	mŏd er ā'tion
mō'tion	e quā'tion	nū mer ā'tion
nō'tion	tes tā'tion	ŏp er ā'tion
pō'tion	for mā'tion	tŏl er ā'tion
pōr'tion	frus trā'tion	trĕp i dā'tion
quō'tient	ḡra dā'tion	văl ū ā'tion

Lesson 131.

Other examples in which final *tion* is pronounced shŭn.

mĕn'tion	ab străe'tion	ĕd ū ea'tion
sĕe'tion	at trăe'tion	ĕm ū lā'tion
frăe'tion	de trăe'tion	ĕx ela mā'tion
dĭe'tion	dis trăe'tion	ĕx pee tā'tion
fĭe'tion	ex.trăe'tion	ĕx pōr tā'tion
frĭe'tion	in frăe'tion	fẽr men tā'tion
jŭne'tion	pro trăe'tion	ġĕn er ā'tion
ăe'tion	re frăe'tion	ḡrăv i tā'tion
eăp'tion	re trăe'tion	hăb i tā'tion
ŏp'tion	eon trăe'tion	ĭl lus trā'tion
făe'tion	sub trăe'tion	ĭm pōr tā'tion

Lesson 132.

Examples in which *sci, ti,* and *ci* have the sound of *sh.*

aɥe'tion	aɥ dā'ciøŭs	ăb er rā'tion
eaɥ'tion	ea pā'ciøŭs	ăd mi rā'tion
eaɥ'tiøŭs	ve rā'ciøŭs	ăd o rā'tion
ḡlā'cial	fal lā'ciøŭs	ăd ū lā'tion
ḡrā'ciøŭs	fu ḡā'ciøŭs	ăḡ ḡra vā'tion
spā'ciøŭs	lo quā'ciøŭs	ăp pli ea'tion
Ḡrē'cian	ra pā'ciøŭs	ăp pro bā'tion
spē'ciøŭs	sa ḡā'ciøŭs	prĕp a rā'tion
pär'tial	te nā'ciøŭs	prĕṣ er vā'tion
eŏn'sciençé	vī vā'ciøŭs	prŏe la mā'tion
spē'cie	vo rā'ciøŭs	prŏf a nā'tion

Lesson 133.

Ci, *ce*, and *si* with the sound of *sh*.

spē'cieş	ju dĭ'cial	aє çĕs'sion
ō'cean	lo ġĭ'cian	єom prĕs'sion
sō'cial	ma ġĭ'cian	de єlĕn'sion
spē'cial	mu şĭ'cian	ex prĕs'sion
єru̧'cial	taє tĭ'cian	im prĕs'sion
prĕ'ciøŭs	op tĭ'cian	op prĕs'sion
păs'sion	pa trĭ'cian	pre tĕn'sion
măn'sion	phў şĭ'cian	suє çĕs'sion
pĕn'sion	pro vĭn'cial	trans ḡrĕs'sion
tĕn'sion	fĭ năn'cial	ad mĭs'sion
tôr'sion	om nĭs'cient	єon єŭs'sion

Lesson 134

Dictation Exercises.

They propose to alter the place of the altar. He cast his ballot for mayor. The ballet dancer and the ballad singer arrived. The wine seller lived in a cellar. He said that the cymbal was a symbol of music. They sent an arrant rogue on the errand. His manner of conducting the manor did not suit the lord. The prophet of Mammon foretold great profit. The relics of the kingdom were saved by the relict of the king. The stature of the statue of Liberty is fixed by statute.

Lesson 135.

răck, *an engine of torture.*
w̵răck, *a sea-plant.*
răp, *to strike.*
w̵răp, *to roll together.*
rĕck, *to heed; to care.*
w̵rĕck, *destruction.*
rīçe̸, *a kind of grain.*
rīse̸, *increase; ascent.*
rīte̸, *a ceremony.*
rīgh̵t, *not wrong.*

w̵rīte̸, *to make letters.*
w̵rīgh̵t, *a workman.*
rōe̸, *eggs of a fish.*
rōw̵, *to impel with oars.*
rōse̸, *a flower.*
rōw̵s, *does row.*
rōe̸s, *plural of roe.*
sēe̸s, *beholds.*   [*water.*
sĕa̸s, *large bodies of*
sei̸ze̸, *to lay hold of.*

Lesson 136.

OF AFFIXES.

Many words are formed by adding something to the end of another word. The added part is called an affix; as *ly*, added to *man*, forms *manly*. In this, and the following seventeen lessons, the more common affixes are indicated.

Plurals formed by adding *s* to the Singular.

rōōfs	sō′lōs̯	tȳ′rōs̯	al bī′nōs̯
hōōfs	hā′lōs̯	jŭn′tōs̯	me mĕn′tōs̯
seärfs	lăs′sōs̯	e̸ăn′tōs̯	oe tä′vōs̯
truths	zē′rōs̯	quạr′tōs̯	sĭ rŏe′e̸ōs̯

Plurals formed by adding *es* to the Singular.

e̸eh̵′ōe̸s̯	to mä′tōe̸s̯	po tä′tōe̸s̯
e̸är′gōe̸s̯	mu lăt′tōe̸s̯	bra vä′dōe̸s̯
mŏt′tōe̸s̯	vol e̸ä′nōe̸s̯	pōr′ti e̸ōe̸s̯
ḡrŏt′tōe̸s̯	môs quï′tōe̸s̯	vī rä′gōe̸s̯

Lesson 137.

Words in which *f* and *fe* are changed into *ves* in the Plural: as, *leaf, leaves; wife, wives.*

beevĕṣ	livĕṣ	thĩevĕṣ	eạ̃lvĕṣ	our sĕlvĕṣ'
shẽạvĕṣ	wīvĕṣ	wọlvĕṣ	hạ̃lvĕṣ	them sĕlvĕṣ'
lẽạvĕṣ	ķnīvĕṣ	lōạvĕṣ	shĕlvĕṣ	yọụr sĕlvĕṣ'

Words in which Y final is changed into *ies* in the Plural.

skīĕṣ	lā'dieṣ	tō'rieṣ	ḡrō'çer ieṣ
spīĕṣ	dū'tieṣ	eăn'dieṣ	fōr'ḡer ieṣ
erīĕṣ	bĕạū'tieṣ	trō'phieṣ	ḡăl'ler ieṣ

Lesson 138.

Words ending in Y which form the Plural by adding *s*.

toyṣ	chĭm'nĕyṣ	ăl'lĕyṣ	at tõr'nĕyṣ
drāyṣ	văl'lĕyṣ	pụl'lĕyṣ	Săt'ur dāyṣ
buọyṣ	mòn'ĕyṣ	tûr'kĕyṣ	hŏl'i dāyṣ
whȳṣ	jọûr'nĕyṣ	mòṇ'kĕyṣ	eôr du royṣ'

Words in which the Plurals are formed irregularly. As the Plural only is given, the teacher might require the pupil to ascertain the Singular, and to spell it.

mīçĕ	erī'sēṣ	tẽr'mi nī	{ kīnĕ
{ stāvĕṣ	chĭl'dren	nĕb'ū læ	{ eowṣ
{ stàffs	{ brŏth'erṣ	a lŭm'nī	{ dīĕṣ
{ pēạ̃sĕ	{ brĕth'ren	vẽr'te bræ	{ dĩçĕ
{ pēạ̃ṣ	strā'tà	syn ŏp'sēṣ	ḡeesĕ

Lesson 139.

Ing signifies *continuing to;* as *talking*, continuing to talk. The following words, in taking their suffix, double the final letter. The last letter is doubled when the word ends with a *single* consonant preceded by a *single* vowel.

plăn′ning	wĭn′ning	stŏp′ping	a bĕt′ting
frĕt′ting	blŏt′ting	ḡŭn′ning	re bĕl′ling
bĭd′ding	rŏb′bing	shŭt′ting	o mĭt′ting

Other words ending with consonants, which do not double the final letter.

ăct′ing	fāɪl′ing	mēạn′ing	ex pănd′ing
lănd′ing	rāɪn′ing	cōạx′ing	con sĕnt′ing
bɏild′ing	sāɪl′ing	sūɪt′ing	vĭṣ′it ing

Lesson 140.

Words ending in *e* silent, generally drop the *e* in adding *ing*.

māk′ing	sēīz′ing	rul′ing	ex pīr′ing
nām′ing	fōrç′ing	līn′ing	re fūṣ′ing
plāgṇ′ing	hĕḍġ′ing	squēez′ing	in trīgṇ′ing
āeḥ′ing	ẇrīt′ing	seḥēm′ing	al lĕġ′ing

The final *e* is retained when it is necessary to prevent a change of pronunciation, or to maintain the identity of a word.

hōẹ′ing	shọẹ′ing	chāngẹ′a blẹ
tōẹ′ing	sīngẹ′ing	trāçẹ′a blẹ
tĭngẹ′ing	dȳẹ′ing	pēạçẹ′a blẹ
fōẹ′man	blūẹ′ness	chärgẹ′a blẹ

Lesson 141.

Ed, as a suffix, generally signifies *did*. In words like the following the *e* in *ed* is silent, and the words, though of two and three syllables, are pronounced in one and two.

blāzẹd	wĕḍġẹd	boilẹd	be rēạvẹd′
drāịnẹd	sŏlvẹd	eoilẹd	be sīēġẹd′
hāīlẹd	eạllẹd	soilẹd	blas phēmẹd′
lāmẹd	haụlẹd	bowẹd	ae quīrẹd′
pāvẹd	maụlẹd	erownẹd	eon trōllẹd′
stōẇẹd	warmẹd	plowẹd	a būṣẹd′
sāvẹd	warnẹd	rouṣẹd	ae eūṣẹd′
fēạrẹd	warpẹd	seourẹd	eom mūnẹd′
flōẇẹd	prọvẹd	sourẹd	eon fūṣẹd′
ḡlūẹd	shŏvẹd	dŏḍġẹd	de eoyẹd′
bĕḡḡẹd	lŏvẹd	fĭllẹd	en joyẹd′

Lesson 142.

In words like the following, *ed* is pronounced as *t;* and, although of two and three syllables, the words are pronounced in one and two.

ḡrāçẹd	fĭxẹd	es ċāpẹd'	at tăckẹd'
sċrāpẹd	mĭxẹd	em brāçẹd'	ċon fĕssẹd'
ċrăckẹd	bŏxẹd	en ḡrōssẹd'	op prĕssẹd'

In other words formed by the affix *ed,* the last letter is doubled in words of one syllable, or in words accented on the last syllable, when they end with a single consonant preceded by a single vowel; as, *wed, wed'ded.* If the word ends in any other consonant than *d* or *t,* the *e* in *ed* becomes silent, and the two syllables become one; as, *hem, hemmed,* pronounced hĕmd.

jŭt'ted	shŭnnẹd	ċom pĕllẹd	o mĭt'tẹd
frĕt'ted	tăppẹd	e quĭppẹd'	im bĕd'ded
fĭt'ted	rŭbbẹd	de mûrrẹd'	ċom mĭt'ted

Lesson 143.

Words not included in the above rule, *do not double* the final consonant.

ăċt'ed	fāị́lẹd	quạr'relẹd	ex pănd'ed
lănd'ed	rāịnẹd	băr'relẹd	mĕr'it ed
rĕst'ed	ċōạxẹd	trăv'elẹd	vĭṣ'it ed

Y is sometimes changed into *i;* as *cry, cried.*

ċrīẹd	drīẹd	măr'riẹd	ḡlō'riẹd
trīẹd	frīẹd	tăr'riẹd	stō'riẹd
shīẹd	spīẹd	ċăr'riẹd	wòr'riẹd

Lesson 144.

Ar, er, and *or* signify *one who does,* or *that which does; as, baker,* one who bakes. If the word ends in *e, r* only is added. After a consonant *y* is generally changed into *i.* Another letter is sometimes united to the affix; as *law, law'yer.* The final consonants are doubled, as in Lesson 142.

bĕg̶'g̶ar	bănk'er	bāk'er	ere ā'tor
dĭg̶'g̶er	plănt'er	pā'çer	eru săd'er
dĭp'per	buïld'er	pāv'er	die tā'tor
elĭp'per	g̶ĭv'er	strān'g̶er	en g̶rāv'er
trŏt'ter	law'yer	writ'er	sur vīv'or
lŏs̟'er	saw'yer	bōa̶st'er	be lĭev'er
wōō'er	rĕa̶d'er	mōu̶rn'er	ad vĭs̟'er
vouch'er	rīd'er	ōwn'er	as sīg̶n'er
wrĕs'ţler	dy̆'er	ru̬l'er	in vĕi̶'g̶ler

Lesson 145.

Words formed by the Affixes *er* or *or*.

be g̶ĭn'ner	lā'bor er	năv'i g̶ā tor
in dôrs'er	rĕa̶'s̟ọn er	dĕd'i ea̶ tor
de s̟ẽrt'er	lĭ'bel er	ea̶l'eu lā tor
dis tûrb'er	wăg̶'on er	spee'ū lā tor
u s̟ûrp'er	eŏn'qu̬er ōr	prŏs'e eū tor
eon dŭet'or	fŏr'ẹig̶n er	eŭl'ti vā tor
tor mĕnt'or	eŭs'tom er	mŭl'ti plī er
en chănt'er	mûr'der er	nū'mer ā tor
sup pŏrt'er	g̶ŏv'ern ōr	g̶ĕn'er ā tor
ag̶ g̶rĕss'or	pĕn'siȯn er	rā'di ā tor

Lesson 146.

In adjectives, *er* is generally added to form the compara-
tive, and *est* to form the superlative; as, *rich, richer, richest.*

strĭct'er	fĭerç'est	wĕalth'i er	wŏr'thi est
brŏad'er	slōw'est	grēed'i er	rĕad'i est
brīght'er	gäunt'est	drĕar'i er	haught'ti est

Ly is an abbreviation of *like;* as *manly* for man-like, or like
a man. *Ly* is still further shortened into *y;* as, *rock, rocky.*

brīght'ly	ĕas'y	hĕav'i ly	thŏr'ough ly
gāy'ly	ĕarth'y	hĕart'i ly	mīght'i ly
nō'bly	spēed'y	rĕad'i ly	hās'ti ly
wĭnd'y	spŏn'ġy	tär'di ly	stĕad'i ly

Lesson 147.

Ness is from the Saxon *nesse,* and means *state* or *quality;* as,
neatness, state of being neat.

blēak'ness	smōōth'ness	còmę'li ness
fĭerçę'ness	nŭmb'ness	drow'şi ness
hōàrsę'ness	wrŏng'ness	naught'i ness
càlm'ness	swēet'ness	wĕa'ri ness

The termination *full* adds its own meaning to the word; as,
joyful, full of joy. The final *l* is omitted in the derivatives..

chānġę'ful	mōurn'ful	skĭll'ful	făn'çi ful
frīght'ful	wōę'ful	wĭll'ful	pĭt'i ful
spītę'ful	wräth'ful	aw'ful	dū'ti ful

Lesson 148.

The termination *less* gives a *negative* meaning to the derivative; as *graceless*, without grace.

brāin'less	sīght'less	frĭend'less	wōrth'less
çēase'less	sōul'less	hĕad'less	house'less
g̅uīle'less	fruit'less	g̅uīlt'less	noise'less

The affix *age* signifies *the pay for, a state of being,* or *composed of;* as *cartage,* the pay for carting.

măr'riage	fĕr'ri age	văg̅'a bŏnd age
hĕrb'age	hēr'mit age	dĭs ad văn'tage
wharf'age	păt'ron age	ĕs'pï on āge

Lesson 149.

The suffix *al* signifies *relating to;* *an* signifies *pertaining to; ant* and *ent,* in many instances, signify the *agent* or *doer.*

tīd'al	ĕom'ie al	me dĭç'i nal
ûr'ban	pŭb'li ean	dī ŏç'e san
ĕlāim'ant	as sĭst'ant	ī tĭn'er ant
ā'gent	prēṣ'i dent	ĕŏr re spŏnd'ent

Able and *ible* signify *that may be, capable of being, fit* or *worthy to be,* or *capacity.*

ēat'a ble	blām'a ble	ăm'i ea ble
sāl'a ble	läugh'a ble	năv'i g̅a ble
lĕg̅'i ble	fōr'çi ble	ĕom bŭs'ti ble
ĕrĕd'i ble	au'di ble	in dĕl'i ble

Lesson 150.

Ist, ster, ee, and *ess,* generally signify the *person who,* or *thing which.* The last is an affix denoting the feminine gender.

aṟr'ist	phy̆ş'i çĭst	pĭ ä'nĭst
tăp'ster	e̶l̶ŏr'is ter	fŏr'est er
g̅rȧnt ēe'	môrt̶ g̅a g̅ēe'	as sĭg̅n ēe'
ĕm'press	shĕp'l̶erd ess	mär'çhĭŏn ess

Dom signifies the *office of* or *state of being; hood, the state of being; ish, somewhat, like;* and *ism,* the *condition* or *doctrines of.*

kĭng'dŏm	e̶l̶rĭs't̶e̶n dŏm	hĕa'th̶e̶n dŏm
chĭld'hŏŏd	mād̶'en hŏŏd	lĭve̶'li hŏŏd
k̶nȧv'ish	yĕl'lōw̶ ish	ā'g̅u ish
Bu̶d'd̶l̶ĭşm	Mĕth'od ĭşm	Môr'mon ĭşm

Lesson 151.

Eer or *ier* generally signifies *one who has charge of; en* means *made of,* or, with adjectives, *to make; ic* signifies *pertaining to, belonging to,* or *like;* and *ise* or *ize, to make, to become,* or *to assimilate.*

e̶ash i̶ēr'	fĭn an çi̶ēr'	g̅ŏn do li̶ēr'
e̶lōth'ier	ĕn g̅i nēer'	e̶ăn non ēer'
bēech'e̶n	be hōld'e̶n	em bōld'e̶n
brĭg̅l̶t'e̶n	en lĭg̅l̶t'e̶n	en lĭv'e̶n
çĭv'ie	çe phăl'ie	me tăl'lie
ū'til īze̶	e̶ăt'e e̶l̶ĭşe̶	e̶rĭt'i çĭşe̶
săt'ir īze̶	çĭv'il īze̶	ŏs'tra çīze̶

Lesson 152.

Ion and *ment* denote *the state of being*, or *the act of; fy, to make* or *become; ance* or *ence, the act* or *state of; ive, having a tendency to,* or *the power* or *nature of; ory, the power* or *nature of,* or *belonging to;* and *ous, partaking of,* or *full of.*

dis pĕr'sion	dĭ vĕr'sion	as pĕr'sion
ex çĕp'tion	e lĕe'tion	ɛon dĭ'tion
a tōnɡ'ment	a ḡrēe'ment	dĕe're ment
dē'i fȳ	stū'pe fȳ	săt'is fȳ
an noy'ançe̸	ae ɛôrd'ançe̸	ɛon ɛôrd'ançe̸
oe ɛŭr'rençe̸	ab hŏr'rençe̸	in dŭl'ɡençe̸
a mū'sĭve̸	ɛon ɛlū'sĭve̸	of fĕn'sĭve̸
ɛûr'so ry	är'mo ry	măn'da to ry
dăn'ɡer o̸ŭs	lĭ'bel o̸ŭs	här mō'ni o̸ŭs

Lesson 153.

Kin, ling, let, and *ule* indicate *smallness* or *diminution.*

lămb̸'kin	măn'i kĭn	lā'dy kĭn
dŭck'ling	ŭn'der ling	fŏs'ter ling
lēaf'let	rĭv'ū let	flăɡ'o̸ lĕt
ḡlŏb'ūle̸	mŏl'e ɛūle̸	ăn i măl'ɛūle̸

Some means *like* or *same, full of,* or *very; ward* denotes *in the direction of; ure* means *state of;* and *y, full of,* or *composed of.*

tīre̸'sŏme̸	ɛŭm'ber sŏme̸	vĕnt'ūre̸ sŏme̸
ēa̸st'ward	hĕa̸v'e̸n ward	åft'er ward
vĕrd'ūre̸	ɛûr'va tūre̸	im pŏst'ūre̸
smōk'y	sĭn'ew y	sĭl'ver y

Lesson 154.

rŭff, *an article of dress.*
rŏŭgh (rŭf), *uneven.*
rĕṭch, *to vomit.* [*son.*
ẉrĕṭch, *a miserable per-*
rōdẹ, *did ride.*
rōạd, *a way; route.*
rōẉẹd, *did row.*
rōōm, *an apartment.*
rḥẹum, *a serous fluid.*
sōẉ, *to scatter seed.*
sew (sō), *to use a needle.*
sō, *thus; in like manner.*

rōạr, *to make a loud noise.*
rōẉ'er, *one who rows.*
sāịl, *a sheet of canvas.*
sālẹ, *the act of selling.*
sēen, *beheld.*
sẹēnẹ, *a view.*
sēịnẹ, *a net for fishing.*
slāỵ, *to kill.* [*ners.*
slẹịgḥ, *a vehicle on run-*
slẹỵ, *a weaver's reed.*
sēem, *to appear.*
sẹạm, *a line of junction.*

Lesson 155.

rụdẹ, *uncivil; rough.*
rōōd, *fourth of an acre.*
sērf, *a slave; servant.*
sûrf, *a swell of the sea.*
sērġẹ, *a kind of cloth.*
sûrġẹ, *to rise; to swell.*
shēer, *pure; clear.*
shēạr, *to cut or clip.*
sīdẹ, *a part; a margin.*
sīgḥẹd, *did sigh.*
slew (slū), *did slay.*
slụẹ, *to slip aside.*

slōẉ, *not fast.*
slōẹ, *a kind of fruit.*
sŭn, *the source of light.*
sòn, *a male child.*
stēel, *refined iron.*
stēạl, *to rob; to pilfer.*
stīlẹ, *steps over a fence.*
stȳlẹ, *manner of writing.*
stârẹ, *to look fixedly.*
stâịr, *a step.* [*taste.*
swēet, *pleasing to the*
suïtẹ (swēt), *retinue.*

Lesson 156.

OF PREFIXES.

When a syllable or word is placed before another word, it is called a prefix. The prefix *re* generally gives the idea of *repetition* or *return ;* as, *recall*, to call back.

rē bŭild′	rē-ap pēạr′	re ăn′i māt𝑒
rē tŏŭch′	rē-as çĕnd′	re ġĕn′er āt𝑒
rē sēạt′	rē-im bûrs𝑒′	re sŭs′çi tāt𝑒
re view′	re dŏŭb′l𝑒	re vēr′ber āt𝑒

The prefix *un* generally gives a *negative* meaning; as, *unapt,* not apt.

un pā𝑖d′	un fr𝑖ĕnd′ly	un ꞓoŭrt′ly
un ꞓlēạn′	un hĕạlth′y	un ēạ′ṣy
un ꞉nōẅn′	un stĕạd′y	un fru𝑖t′fụl
un nērv𝑒′	un ĕrr′ing	un lĕạrn′ed

Lesson 157.

In, also, has a negative meaning; it often becomes *im*, *il*, *ir*, or *ig*, for the sake of sound.

in ăꞓt′ĭv𝑒	ĭn sin çĕr𝑒′	ir rĕṣ′o lūt𝑒
im prŏp′er	ĭm po līt𝑒′	ĭr re liġ′𝑖ŏŭs
il lē′ġal	il lū′sĭv𝑒	ĭr re spĕꞓt′ĭv𝑒
iġ nō′bl𝑒	ĭġ′no rant	ĭr′ri ta bl𝑒

ĭm ma tē ri ăl′i ty	im prăꞓ ti ꞓa bĭl′i ty
ĭn dĭ vĭṣ i bĭl′i ty	ĭn de strŭꞓ ti bĭl′i ty
ĭn ꞓom păt i bĭl′i ty	ĭr re ṣĭst i bĭl′i ty
ĭn ꞓom prĕss i bĭl′i ty	im pĕn e tra bĭl′i ty

Lesson 158.

Dis is a Latin particle, and has the force of a *negative* or *privative*; as, *disagree*, not to agree, *disarm*, to deprive of arms.

dis plē*a̸*s*e̸*′   dĭs ap pē*a̸*r′   dĭs ¢on tĭn′ū*e̸*
dis joint′   dĭs be l*i̸*ēv*e̸*′   dĭs in hĕr′it
dis lŏ*d̸*g*e̸*′   dĭs o blī*ḡe̸*′   dis ôr′ḡan īz*e̸*
dis chärg*e̸*′   dis ¢*ø*ŭr′ag*e̸*   dis sĭm′i lar
dis ḡrā¢*e̸*′   dis ¢ŏv′er   dis ¢rĭm′i nāt*e̸*

The prefix *after* conveys its own meaning.

àft′er p*i̸*ē¢*e̸*   àft′er nōōn   àft′er mōst
àft′er ḡ*µ*ärd   àft′er măth   àft′er-thô*µ*g*h̸*t

Lesson 159.

Post is a Latin word, meaning *after.*

pōst′s¢rĭpt   pōst-dĭ lū′vi an   pōst me rĭd′i an
pōst′-dāt*e̸*   pōst po s*i̸*′tion   pŏst′hu m*ø*ŭs ly

Other words are formed by prefixing the English word *post*, a letter-carrier.

pōst′al   pōst′man   pōst′märk
pōst′-chā*i̸*s*e̸*   pōst′-town   pōst′-ŏf f*i̸*¢*e̸*
pōst-hāst*e̸*′   pōst′boy   pōst′màs ter

Bene is a Latin prefix, signifying *well.*

bĕn′ө dĭet   bĕn e fă¢′tion   be nĕf′i çen¢*e̸*
bĕn′e f*i̸*¢*e̸*   bĕn e fĭ′cial   be nĕv′o len¢*e̸*

Lesson 160.

Fore adds its own meaning to the word; as *foretaste*, to taste before; *pre* is from the Latin *præ*, before; *ante* (Latin), before. *Anti* (Greek), means *against* or *opposite.*

fōre′sīght	fōre tĕll′er	fōre bŏd′ing ly
fōre′mōst	fōre knŏwl′edge	fōre de tẽr′mĭne
fōre knōw′	fōre′eas tle	pre mĕd′i tāte
pre fīx′	pre eau′tion	pre ŏe′eu pȳ
pre jŭdge′	pre çĕd′ing	pre-ĕm′i nent
pre sẽrve′	pre dĕs′tĭne	ăn te păs′eħal
pre sāge′	ăn′te păst	ăn te mŭn′dāne
pre tĕxt′	ăn′te dāte	ăn te nŭp′tial
fōre warn′	ăn′tĭ pōde	ăn tĭ eli′max
fōre′frŏnt	ăn′tĭ dōte	ăn tĭ fĕb′rĭle

Lesson 161.

The word *miss* signifies *to err, to go wrong;* in the compound the last *s* is omitted.

mis gŭíde′	mĭs be lĭef′	mis rĕck′ŏn
mis spĕll′	mĭs eon çĕíve′	mis eŏn′strue
mis chōōṣe′	mĭs dĭ rĕet′	mis ḡŏv′ern
mis chănçe′	mĭs re çīte′	mis ḡŭíd′ançe

Words formed by the prefixes *up* and *under.*

up rāíṣe′	ŭn der lāy′	ŭn′der hănd
up hĕáve′	ŭn der wrīte′	ŭn′der ḡrōwth
ŭp′rīght	ŭn der sīgn′	ŭn′der brŭsh
ŭp′ward	ŭn der nēáth′	ŭn′der shŏt

Lesson 162.

Words formed by the prefixes *out* and *over*.

out brāvₑ'	ō ver rēₐch'	ō'ver bōₐrd
out ḡrōw'	ō ver aw̶ₑ'	ō'ver ₐllṣ
out pōᵤr'	ō ver flōw'	ō'ver nīg̶h̶t
out tₐ̣lk'	ō ver freīg̶h̶t'	ō'ver sīg̶h̶t

Counter, from the Latin *contra,* against.

₵oun'ter pānₑ	₵oun'ter sīg̶n	₵oun ter mₒvₑ'
₵oun'ter f̶ₑit	₵oun'ter point	₵oun ter weīg̶h̶'

Extra (Latin), *beyond.*

ĕx tra ju dĭ'cial	ĕx tra phỵ̇ṣ'i₵ al
ĕx tra pro vĭn'cial	ĕx tra trŏp'i₵ al

Lesson 163.

Semi (Latin), and *hemi* (Greek), half; *super* (Latin), over or above; *trans* (Latin), beyond or through; and *inter* (Latin), among or between.

sĕm'i brēvₑ	sĕm'ĭ ₵ō lon	sĕm'ĭ quā ver
ˢsĕm'ĭ tōnₑ	sĕm'ĭ çīr ₵lₑ	sĕm ĭ tŏn'iₑ
hĕm'i sphērₑ	hĕm'ĭ çẏ ₵lₑ	hĕm i môrph'iₑ
hĕm'i trŏpₑ	hĕm i hē'dral	hĕm i sphĕr'iₑ
sū per ădd'	sū per fĭ'cial	sū per in dū₵ₑ'
sū per s₵rībₑ'	su pẽr'flu ₵ŭs	sū per strŭ₵t'ūrₑ
tran s₵ĕnd'ent	trăns at lăn'tiₑ	trăn'si to ry
trans fĭḡ'ūrₑ	trans fūṣ'i blₑ	trans mĭs'si blₑ
ĭn'ter ₵ōᵤrsₑ	ĭn ter mĭt'tent	ĭn ter rĕḡ'num
ĭn'ter lūdₑ	ĭn ter çĕs'sor	ĭn ter sĕₑ'tion

Lesson 164.

Ad signifies *to*, and for euphony takes the forms of *ac, af, ag, al, an, ap, ar,* and *as;* as *ad* and *verto, advert,* to turn to.

ad dūçe′	al lūre′	as sāi̇l′	ăḡ′ḡre ḡāte
ae eount′	an nĕx′	ad vànçe′	ăḡ′ḡra vāte
ae eôrd′	ar rīve′	ăd′vẽrb	ap pĕnd′aḡe
af fĭx′	as çĕnd′	ăd′vẽrse	ăr′ro ḡançe

Bi (from Latin *bis*, twice) means *two, double,* or *in two.*

bī′fid	bī dĕn′tate	bī nō′mi al
bī′fôrm	bī eôr′nøŭs	bī ĕn′ni al
bī′nate	bī fûr′eate	bī nŏe′ū lar
bī′ped	bī lĭṇ′ḡual	bī vălv′ū lar
bī sĕet′	bī pär′tīte	bī sŭl′phu ret

Lesson 165.

Con (Latin *cum*, with) signifies *with* or *together;* it takes the forms of *com, col, co, cog,* and *cor,* for ease in pronunciation.

eon vẽrt′	eŏn de sçĕnd′	eon vĕn′tion al
eom prĕss′	eom păn′ion	eŏm pen sā′tion
eol lĕet′	eŏl′lo quy	eol lăt′er al
eo hēre′	eō-ex ĭst′	eō-ex tĕn′sive
eŏḡ′nāte	eŏḡ′nĭ zant	eoḡ nŏs′çi ble
eor rĕet′	eŏr re spŏnd′	eŏr o nā′tion
eon eûr′	eon vŭl′sion	eon sĕe′ū tive
eon dīḡn′	eon vey′er	eŏn se quĕn′tial
eon fôrm′	eon tū′şion	eon năt′ū ral

Lesson 166.

De signifies *down* or *from*; *epi* signifies *on, near, during*; and *ex* has the meaning *out of*. *Ex* also becomes *e, ec,* or *ef*.

de sçĕnd′	ex trăet′	ĕp i dĕm′ie
de trăet′	e vādę′	ĕp′i lĕp sy
de nōtę′	ef fūsę′	ĕp i ḡlŏt′tis
de vōtę′	ĕe′lŏḡuę	ĕp i dĕrm′is

Dis, ob, per, and *circum* mean respectively *apart, against, through,* and *around*. With English words, *dis* gives a *negative* meaning.

dis tĕnd′	dis sĕv′er	dĭs em bär′rass
ob trudę′	ob liquę′ly	ob lĭt′er ātę
per plĕx′	per fĕet′ĭvę	per sĭst′en çy
çĭr′euit	çĭr eum vŏlvę′	çĭr eum jā′çent

Lesson 167.

Mal signifies *evil, ill; mono* is from Greek *monos, single; pan* (Greek), signifies *all, every thing;* and *poly* (Greek *polus*), *many.*

măl'ᴇon tĕnt	ma lĭ'ciø̆ŭs	ma lĕv'o lent
mŏn'o tōnǥ	mŏn'o ḡrăm	mo nŏp'o ly
păn'o ply	păn'the ĭst	păn o rä'mȧ
pŏl'y ḡŏn	pŏl'y pŭs	pŏl'y thē ĭṣm

Pro is a Latin preposition signifying *for, before,* and *forth; uni* (Latin *unus, one*) signifies *one* or *producing one; syn* (sometimes *syl* and *sym*) signifies *together;* and *sub* (sometimes *suf, sup,* and *sug*) denotes *under, below.*

prō'noun	ū'ni ty	sȳn'the sĭs	sub sᴇrībǥ'
pro pĕl'	ū'ni fôrm	sȳl'la blǥ	sŭf'fĭx
pro dūçǥ'	ū'ni ᴇôrn	sȳm'pa thy	sup prĕss'
pro vīdǥ'	ū'ni vălvǥ	sȳn tăᴇ'tiᴇ	suḡ ḡĕst'

Lesson 168.

Compound Words promiscuously arranged.

ālǥ'-housǥ	līmǥ'-kĭlṇ	hĕḏḡǥ'hŏḡ
hāḭl'stōnǥ	bōȧt'man	pĕn'ᴋnīfǥ
lāy'man	fōu̇r'seōrǥ	ḡrĭst'-mĭll
sāfǥ'ḡu̇ärd	lōȧd'stōnǥ	mĭd'nīḡht
wāḭst'ᴇōȧt	ōȧt'mēȧl	pĭ̱ch'fôrk
bēe'-hīvǥ	pōlǥ'-stär	shĭp'ẇrĕck
kēy'-stōnǥ	snōẇ'-drŏp	ẇrist'band
ᴋnēe'-păn	spōrts'man	blŏck'hĕȧd
brīdǥ'ḡrōōm	jew'ṣ'-härp	ᴇrŏss'-bōẇ
lĭḡht'-housǥ	lūkǥ'wa̤rm	ŏff'sprĭng

Lesson 169.

Compound Words.

Lĭsle̸-ḡlȯve̸	nīgh̸t'fạll	härts'hôrn
nôrth-ēạst'	bŏŏk'-eāse̸	ċôrn'-staḷk
joint'-stŏck	fŏŏt'stōol	lōōp'-hōle̸
wĕll'-brĕd	ċôrk'serew	bûr'dŏck
snŭff'-bŏx	wạtch'-wŏrd	whĭrl'pōōl
towns̠'man	brōōm'stĭck	fōōls̠'ċăp
house̸'wife̸	dōōms̠'dāy̸	wŏrk'shŏp
chär'ċōạl	brown'-brĕạd	for sōōth'
out weịgh'	down'rīgh̸t	down'eạst
hôrn'pīpe̸	tōōth'āċhe̸	nōōn'dāy̸
hēịr'lōōm	âịr' brāke̸	laẉ'sūịt

Lesson 170.

Compound Words.

ċăn'dle̸ stĭck	pōst'al-ċärd	bŭt'ter flȳ
hănd'ker chịẹf	ċŏp'y-bŏŏk	wạ'ter-fạll
bĕd'-chām ber	ŏft̸'ẹn tīme̸s̠	ḡăs'-mē ter
ĕv'er ḡrēen	tȳpe̸'-ẉrīt er	ċlēr'ġy̸ man
ġĕn'tle̸ man	jȯûr'ne̸y̸ man	brĭċ'-a-bràċ
pĕp'per mĭnt	hŭm'ming-bīrd	nā'vy̸-yärd
ċămp'-mēet ing	mŭsk'-mĕl on	fōōl'-härd y
màs'ter pịēċe̸	blȯŏd'-vĕs sel	ạl mīgh̸t'y
pàss'ō ver	hŏn'e̸y̸-ċōmb̸	bȳ'stănd er
fowl'ing-pịēċe̸	stĕm'-wīnd er	bàss'-vī ol
pow'der-hôrn	seh̸ōōl'-màs ter	tāle̸'-be̸âr er

Lesson 171.

SYNTHETIC AND DICTATION EXERCISES.

Ā'bel, *a man's name.*
a'blḙ, *powerful.*
ăl'lḙy, *a narrow passage.*
al lȳ', *one who assists.*
ăl lū'ṣion, *a reference.*
ĭl lū'ṣion, *mockery.*
de sçĕnd'ant, *offspring.*

de sçĕnd'ent, *falling.*
eôu̇gh'er, *one who coughs.*
eŏf'fer, *a chest.* [*sugar.*
eăn'diḙd, *covered with*
eăn'did, *honest; truthful.*
çĕnt'ū ry, *100 years.*
sĕn'try, *a guard.*

The able man's name was Abel. A narrow alley. France was an ally of England in the Crimean war. He made an allusion to the illusion that possessed him. His descendant was descendent from the same line. The cougher sat on the coffer. The candid youth ate the candied cakes. The sentry wore a costume of the last century.

Lesson 172.

Words spelled alike, whose Pronunciation and Meaning differ.

āyḙ, *always.*
äy̆ḙ, *an affirmative vote.*
chōṣḙ, *did choose.*
çhōṣḙ, *a thing; a chattel.*
bāss, *a term in music.*
bȧss, *a fish.*
eon jūrḙ', *to implore.*

eȯn'jurḙ, *to enchant.*
bōw̆, *a weapon.*
bow, *part of a ship.*
chăp, *a boy.*
chȧp, *the jaw.*
ḡout, *a disease.*
ḡou̇t́, *taste; relish.*

Lesson 173.

Words spelled alike, whose Pronunciation and Meaning differ.

mäll, *a public walk.*

mạll, *a mallet.* [*skin.*

sløŭgh (slŭf), *a snake's*

slougĥ, *a miry place.*

wĕạr, *a dam in a river.*

wǿâr, *waste.* [*seconds.*

mĭn'utǿ (mĭn'it), *sixty*

mĭ nūtǿ', *very small.*

hīnd'er, *in the rear.*

hĭn'der, *to obstruct.*

seạld, *a burn.*

seăld, *a poet.* [*sews.*

sew'er (sō'er), *one who*

sew'er (sū'er), *a drain.*

eǿûrt'e sy, *civility.*

eǿûrtǿ'sy, *a slight bow.*

slāv'er, *a slave ship.*

slăv'er, *spittle.*

ī'ron y (ī'urn ў), *of iron.*

ī'ron y, *ridicule.*

woŗst'ed, *a kind of yarn.*

wŏrst'ed, *defeated.*

Lesson 174.

Words in which the letter A is often mispronounced. Some of the words in this and succeeding lessons have two pronunciations, but in all cases the preferable one is given.

hǿärth	mam mä'	ān'cient	frā'ter nizǿ
ḡrȧss	a slȧnt'	lā'vȧ	eŏm man dänt'
slȧnt	pa pä'	säŋn'ter	tī ā'rȧ
ḡäpǿ	a lȧs'	pạl'frǿў	ăl tēr'natǿ
ḡäŋnt	äĺ'mȯnd	răp'inǿ	af flā'tus
fär	seăth'less	drä'mȧ	hī ā'tus
swäthǿ	păg'eạnt	lā'mȧ	ba nä'nȧ
lȧnçǿ	stạl'wart	dā'tȧ	sul tā'nȧ
eäĺm	ȧft'er	mä'ği	man dā'mus
läŋgh	pâr'ent	pā'thos	oe tā'vo

Lesson 175.

Words in which A is frequently mispronounced.

chăl'drŏn	ar ęā'num	u rā'ni ŭm
nā'tant	er rā'tum	a quā'ri ŭm
hạl'berd	ver bā'tim	ăp pa rā'tus
tăs'sel	văl'en tīnę	ĭḡ no rā'mus
saṉ'çy	ęā'ri ǫus	ir ră'tion al
mãęl'strŏm	trā'eḥe à	lĭt er ā'tī
squā'lôr	bär băr'ie	lĭt er ā'tim
dại'ry	băr ri ęādę'	ŭl ti mā'tum
ęā'ret	rā'di ŭs	măr a năth'à
ḡrā'tis	eḥŏl'e rà	ġym nā'şi ŭm
rā'dix	ęa nā'ry	ex pā'ti ātę

Lesson 176.

Sounds of A frequently mispronounced.

ḡlā'moυr	săę'ra ment	ḡlànçę	ạl'wāўş
ràft'er	ā'pri ęŏt	zǫuävę	a màss'
sęạl'lŏp	ḡär'rụ lǫus	drăịn	Ăr'ab
ęrâft'y	bra vā'do	stànch	bā'thos
ḡràss'y	de făl'ęātę	sęârçę	ęạl'drŏn
em bä/m'	ęa ęā'o	ęănt	chäs'ṭęn
a ḡḥäst'	răị/l'ler y	ęän't	fäç'ĭlę
wạs'sạil	an dăn'te	străp	fàịr'y
bä/m'ў	hạl'i but	yạęḥt	ḡā'là
ạl'der	nä'ïvę tẹ	seăth	quä'sī
Ăl'dīnę	fï nä'lẹ	ęạ/k	lo ęälę'

Lesson 177.

Sounds of A often mispronounced.

swạth	pạu̶'per	ḡra vā'men	ā mĕn'
hä̱l̶v̶	hā'rem	to mā'to	ḡuä'no
j̶ēan	pa shạ'	sā'li ent	nä'ïv̶
ҽä̱ch	fắç'et	pä'ri ạ̶	här'ass
bä̱m	fạl'ch̶i̶ŏn	far rā'ḡo	sặt'īr̶
ḡrø̶at	läu̶gh'ter	tăp'es try	jăl'ap
trànç̶	tăr'iff	de ҽā'denç̶	e ҽlä̱'
y̶ēā	ba sạlt'	ā're ȧ	prāi̶'ri̶e
är̶	hụr rä'	va ḡā'ry	rā'tion
shȧft	bä tōṉ'	ҽū'po lȧ	Săl'iҽ
seâr̶d	quăḡ'mīr̶	ҽu rā'tor	tā'pis

Lesson 178.

Words in which the Sounds of E are often mispronounced.

ē̶i̶'ther	ĕq'ui ty	lĕḡ'end a ry
prē'çept	tĕn'a bl̶	ab stē'mi ø̶ŭs
wĕ̶ap'ø̶n	ē'ḡo tĭ̱m	a mē'na bl̶
prĕl'at̶	tĕr'ra pĭn	a pē'ri ent
yĕl'lōw̶	al lҽ'ḡro	stē're o tȳp̶
vĕn dū̶'	in hēr'ent	săҽ ri lē'ḡi̶ø̶ŭs
for ḡĕt'	lē'ni ent	be nĕf'i çent
stē̶ad'y	yĕs'ter dạȳ	a mĕn'i ty
ĕn'ḡin̶	ē'qua bl̶	e lē'ḡi aҽ
kĕt'tl̶	pē'o ny	hȳ men ē'al
trĕb'l̶	ē'qui poi̶̱	ĕm py rē'an

Lesson 179.

Words in which the Sounds of E are often mispronounced.

lĕ̇ant	pĕt'rel	çērø'ment	les sēe'
drĕ̇amt	sē'rĭes	lĕĭ'surø	mẹ lẹø'
êyrø	sĕam'stress	ef fētø'	dĕ̇af'øn
rĕ̇ar	stēel'yard	en fĕøff'	rọu e'
dĕ̇af	sĕx'ton	kĕ̇øl'sȯn	ẹ lĭtø'
tĕ̇at	fē'brĭlø	sĕck'øl	kḥẹ dïvø'
pērt	fĕe'und	bĕs'tial	rĕs'pĭtø
tẹtø	sĕn'nȧ	fĕt'id	thêrø'förø
fĕøff	tĕn'et	fē'tiçh	prĕf'açø
ĕg̃g	tĕp'id	sē'nĭlø	tĕt'ter
yĕt	lē'ver	hē'lot	mĕt'riє

Lesson 180.

Words in which the Sounds of E are often mispronounced.

pĕr'ukø	nĕp'o tĭşm	tĕr'ri blø
nĕth'er	as çĕt'iє	rĕş'in øŭs
pĕt'al	rĕd'o lent	rĕç'i pē
rĕş'in	єō te rĭē'	tĕt'a nŭs
ra çēmø'	ĕm ploy ẹ'	rĕf'lu ent
prē'lūdø	ăt ta çhẹ'	hȳ ē'mal
mē'grim	prē'mi er	çĕr'e brŭm
vĕn'ūø	o bĕĭ'sançø	vē'he ment
bre vĕt'	g̃ĕn'er ȧ	dĕf'i çit
єär tĕl'	Ma dĕĭ'rȧ	splĕn'e tiє
ē'pă̇et	hĕr'o ĭnø	ī dē'ȧ

Lesson 181.

Words in which the Sounds of I are often mispronounced.

fī′nīt¢	mēr′ean tīl¢	pa rī′e̊ tal
prō′fil¢	pĭ ăz′zà	rĕç i ta tīv¢′
de brĭş′	he ġī′rà	an nī′hi lāt¢
Ā′pril	de eli′vø̸ŭs	eăl lī′o pe
fĭ nănç¢′	O rī′on	he lī′ae al
ŏx′ĭd¢	ĭ tăl′ie	zo dī′ae al
är′eḥīv¢ş	ho rī′zon	ī sŏeḥ′ro nø̸ŭs
vĭş′or	sī′ne eūr¢	mĕn in ġī′tis
sĭr′up	sō rī′tēş	ma nī′ae al
bas tīl¢′	brŏn eḥī′tis	seär la tĭ′nà
rĭb′ald	trĭp′ar tīt¢	ī so thĕrm′al

Lesson 182.

Words in which the Sounds of I are often mispronounced.

rĭd	tĭ rād¢′	pў̆ rī′tēş
vīv¢	ton tīn¢′	fa rī′nà
rĭns¢	brō′mĭn¢	măr′i tĭm¢
shīr¢	lī′eḥen	pĭ ä′no
wĭdth	ob lïqu̸¢′	vĭr′ṵ lent
sī′ren	vĭş′eount	çў̆n′o su̦r¢
tĭ′ny	vī′rĭl¢	ĭs′o lāt¢
lĭ′en	spīk¢′nard	vŏl′a tĭl¢
ăn′īl¢	trĭb′ūn¢	en frăn′chĭş¢
¢ī′der	quī′nīn¢	de çī′sĭv¢
trī′ō	dĭ lāt¢′	pū′er ĭl¢

Lesson 183.

Words in which the Sounds of I are often mispronounced.

fū'tĭl/e	as pīr'ant	ăd ver tīṣ'er
är tĭst/e'	in quīr'y	trĭ sўl'la bl/e
fĭ nĕss/e'	sub sĭd'enç/e	ka l/ī'do sĕōp/e
stĭr'rup	chăs'tĭṣ/e ment	ad vēr'tĭṣ/e ment
sŭb'tĭl/e	dĭ grĕs'sion	in ter nē'çīn/e
e/lō'rīn/e	dĭ mĕn'sion	lăr yn ġī'tis
Ăl'pīn/e	dĭ plō'má	mĭ răe'ū l/ŭs
çhï eān/e'	sĭm'o ny	in çī'so ry
euï ṣīn/e'	erĭn'o lin/e	vī vĭp'a r/ŭs
lĭ'lae	păr'a dĭġm	ĭs o lā'tion
vĭe'ar	e e/ī'nŭs	sī mul tā'ne /ŭs

Lesson 184.

Words in which O is sometimes mispronounced.

hō/m	trō'phy	mŏn'as ter y
yōlk	ōn'ly	prŏe'ū rā tor
sĕŏff	mó<u>n</u>'ḡrel	mī erŏs'eo py
nŏnç/e	be trŏth'	drŏm'e da ry
eŏst	prŏç'ess	zo ŏl'o ġy
wōn't	dŏç'ĭl/e	al lŏp'a thy
wŏnt	prŏv'ŏst	a/ tŏm'a ton
shōn/e	ḡrŏv'/el	hȳ drŏp'a thy
slŏth	fŏr/e'/éa/d	La ŏe'o ŏn
fōrḡ/e	jŏe'und	pho tŏġ'ra phy
dŏth	dŏ<u>n</u>'k/ey	ĭn ter lŏe'ū tor

Lesson 185.

Words in which O is sometimes mispronounced.

frŏnt'ĭer   ăp ro pōs'   ab dō'men
plŏv'er   vō'ea blė   dis €ŏm'fit
a moŭr'   pōs tĭl'ion   €øûrt'e øŭs
hŏv'er   pre €ō'ciøŭs   pa rŏt'id
sur toŭt'   ō'o lĭtė   €on dō'lençė
slŏth'ful   dŏl'or øŭs   €oḡ nō'men
Soŭ çhŏng'   €a lŏr'ie   op pō'nent
€øoŭṭ'choŭe   frŏnt'is pĭēçė   €o rō'nȧ
re vōlt'   prŏb'i ty   €ŏl'pōrt ėur
fôrt'nīḡht   pȯmė ḡrăn'atė   pō'ta blė
€ȯm'pass   sȯv'er øiḡn   a rō'mȧ

Lesson 186.

Words in which U is sometimes mispronounced.

tṵllė   €ŏl'umṵ   in aṵ'ḡu rātė
jøŭst   sūt'ūrė   çe rṵ'le an
ḡṵīdė   pŭp'pet   vī tū'per ātė
yoŭrş   sṵ'mae   ae €ū'mu lātė
ḡŭoŭl   fŭl'sȯmė   €ō ad jū'tor
ḡĭȧour   €ŏn'dŭit   pū'pil la ry
de bṵṭ'   €ū'€um ber   ĭn'sti tūtė
dŭe'at   trṵ'eu lent   øū rē'kȧ
Ū'lan   €ŏn nøis sėṵr'   çæ şū'rȧ
sŭp'plė   jū'ḡu lar   €ŏn'sti tūtė
dū'ty   nū'mer øŭs   tøûr'na ment

Lesson 187.

Words properly accented on the first Syllable.

eŏn'strŭȼ	eŏm'bat ant	pū'is sançȼ
trăv'ersȼ	dĭs'pu tant	ĭn'ter ĭm
rămp'ant	ḡŏn'do lȧ	ąu'top sy
ăth'lētȼ	plĕth'o rȧ	tȳm'pa nŭm
sȳr'ingȼ	mĭs'chȉev øŭs	wĭsȼ'ā erȼ
ĕx'tant	blăs'phe møŭs	ôr'eȼes tral
brīg'and	eŏn'ver sant	ĭm'po tent
eŏn'ȼôrd	săn'he drĭm	eŏn'ḡrŭ ent
dĭs'ȼôrd	eŏn'tra ry	ĭm'be çĭlȼ
dō'nātȼ	prō'te an	phā'e tŏn
ŏb'long	dĭs'ȼi plĭnȼ	rĕt'i nȧ

Lesson 188.

rōll, *to turn over and over.*
rōlȼ, *a part performed.*
sīgn, *a token; a mark.*
sīnȼ, *a line in geometry.*
skŭll, *part of the head.*
seŭll, *to impel a boat.*
slēevȼ, *an arm cover.*
slĕȧvȼ, *untwisted silk.*
slīght, *to neglect; feeble.*
slȼīght, *dexterity.*
soµl, *the immortal spirit.*
sōlȼ, *bottom of the foot.*
sōrȼ, *a hurt; painful.*

sōạr, *to mount upward.*
stākȼ, *a pointed stick.*
stȼāk, *a slice of flesh.*
stĕp, *a pace; a foot-print.*
stĕppȼ, *a dreary plain.*
stōōp, *to bend forward.*
stoµp, *a basin; a pitcher.*
sŭm, *the amount; whole.*
sȯmȼ, *a part; a portion.*
tālȼ, *that which is told.*
tāȉl, *terminal appendage.*
târȼ, *allowance in weight.*
tȼâr, *to rend; to lacerate.*

Lesson 189.

tăcks, *small nails.*
tăx, *import; duty.*
thrōnͤ, *seat of a king.*
thrōẃn, *cast.* [*gether.*
tēạm, *horses hitched to-*
tēem, *to bring forth.*
tēạr, *water from the eye.*
tiͤr, *a row or rank.*
threw (thru̱), *did throw.*
thro̤u̱gh, *from end to end.*
tīmͤ, *duration.*
thͫȳmͤ, *a pungent herb.*

tōͤ, *part of the foot.*
tōẃ, *coarse part of flax.*
trăet, *a region.*
trăckͤd, *followed.*
thēͥr, *belonging to them.*
thêrͤ, *in that place.*
thrōẃ, *to cast; to hurl.*
thrōͤ, *agony.*
tīdͤ, *rising of the sea.*
tiͤd, *bound; fastened.*
tōạd, *a harmless reptile.*
tōẃͤd, *drawn by a rope.*

Lesson 190.

Words properly accented on the first Syllable.

prŏḡ'ress
ĭn'ḡrātͤ
pǣ'an
eo̤n'pŏn̲
dū'ress
ḡŏŏd'măn
ō'zōnͤ
ā'eorn
prō'lŏḡu̇ͤ
thīr'tēen
sär'dĭnͤ

ĕq'ui paḡͤ
phŏs'phor ŭs
lū'di eroͤŭs
vĭç'i naḡͤ
ĭn'te ḡral
ĭn'te ḡer
ăn'çes tor
ăn'tĭ pōdͤs̲
ăt'ro phy
eŏm'plaͥ s̲ant
dĕt'o nātͤ

ĕx'qui s̲ĭtͤ ly
eŏm'pa ra blͤ
pĕr'emp to ry
ôr'tho e py
ĕx̲'em pla ry
lăm'en ta blͤ
ĭn'ter ĕst ing
eŏn'tu me ly
sŭb'lu na ry
vā'ri o loid
ē'ti o lātͤ

Sp. **8.**

Lesson 191.

Words properly accented on the second Syllable.

trust ēe′	he răl′die	ap pĕl′la tĭvҽ
mon sōōn′	ple thŏr′ie	a nĕm′o ne
pro lĭx′	re ҽū′şant	är tĭf′ĭ çer
băck slīdҽ′	ple bē′ian	är bĭt′ra ment
whêrҽ ăş′	pre çĕd′ençҽ	ҽon sŭm′matҽ ly
ḡā¡n sāy′	le thē′an	ҽa mĕl′o pard
re çess′	il lŭs′trātҽ	ҽon nŏt′a tĭvҽ
pla ҽärd′	im mŏb′ilҽ	in tēr′po lātҽ
a dĕpt′	phĭ lip′pie	te lĕḡ′ra phy
suҽ çess′	o dē′on	pe rĭph′ra sĭs
ro mănçҽ′	e lā′inҽ	re ҽŏn′nais sänçҽ

Lesson 192.

Words properly accented on the second Syllable.

eos tūmé'   so nō'réŭs   re mĕd'i less
with drạẃ'   lȳ çĕ'um   pre çĕd'en çy
sue çịṉet'   mu ṣē'um   hȳ pẽr'bo le
ex çĕss'   e nẽr'vāté   py răm'i dal
de fuṉet'   ae elī'māté   te lĕph'o ny
ea nīné'   in ŭn'dāté   il lŭs'tra tïvé
mo rälé'   eon dĕn'sāté   ex ĕe'ū tor
re läẏ'   Lin næ'an   ex tĕm'po re
sĭ mōōm'   ŏb jûr'ḡāté   ḡla dī'o lŭs
re eōúrsé'   ad ŭm'brāté   in fĕr'a blé
ae çĕss'   eẖo rē'us   eẖal çĕd'o ny

Lesson 193.

Words properly accented on the second Syllable.

ex trạôr'di na ry   in tẽr'po lä tor
in eŏm'på ra blé   eon sŏl'a to ry
ir rĕf'ra ḡa blé   de līb'er a tïvé
ir rĕp'a ra blé   pro thŏn'o ta ry
ir rĕv'o ea blé   dis erĭm'i na tïvé
in dĭs'so lu blé   eom mĕm'o ra tïvé
in dĭs'pu ta blé   ae çĕl'er a tïvé
in ĕx'o ra blé   sa lū'ta to ry
ab sŏl'ū to ry   pa rī'e ta ry
de mŏn'stra tïvé ly   nun eū'pa to ry
oe tŏǧ'e na ry   in ĕx'pli ea blé

Lesson 194.

Words properly accented on the third Syllable.

rĕv er ĭe′	ăm a tọ̤ur′	dĕm o nī′a̤e al
ŏb li ḡôr′	bȯm ba zĭnḡ′	hō me ŏp′a thy
jăḡ ū är′	tăm bọur ĭnḡ′	ăp o thē′o sis
ĭm pro vīṣe′	rĭe o çhĕt′*	hĕr e dĭt′a ment
ôr mo lṳ′	mū le tēer′	spŏn ta nē′i ty
ĕt ĭ qu̶ĕtte′	ma̤u̶ so lē′um	ĕp i zō′o ty
ăv a lănçhe′	e̤ŏn ser vā′tor	hȳ per bō′re an
ăs sĭḡn ôr′	e̤ŏt y lē′don	ĕp i e̤ū′re an
pō lo nä̤ịṣe′	nō men e̤lāt′ūre	Pȳth a ḡō′re an
e̤ăt a fălqu̶e′	hȳ men ē′an	hĭp po pŏt′a mŭs
dĭs ḥa bĭlle′	dĕn ū dā′tion	rĕç ĭ prŏç′ĭ ty

Lesson 195.

Words frequently mispronounced, or improperly accented.

mŭlet	sā′chem	jăve′lin	hŏs′t̶ler
soͦot	ăstḥ′mà	chĕst′nut	dē′tä̤il*
nooͦṣe	lē′ḡend	w̶rĕs′t̶le	fa çāde′
twiçe	de sĭḡn′*	ôr′eḥis	strȳeḥ′nĭne
nĭche	ĭstḥ′mus	lĭst′en	pĕr′fūme*
sä̤lve	thĭs′t̶le	ba̤ȳ′o̤u̶	mus täçhe′
hei̤ḡht	rä̤i′ṣĭn	ḡĭb′bo̤ŭs	bȧs′ket
mĭlch	a dŭlt′	ḡlä′çĭer	Ḡäḡ′lie
browṣe*	ṗsälm′ist	ḡrĭev′o̤ŭs	Le vănt′*
vāṣe	ŏft′en	nä′ṣal	sŏft′en

* As a noun.

Lesson 196.

Words frequently mispronounced, or improperly accented.

though	goose'ber ry	da guerre'o type
gist	sooth'say er	cab ri o let'
fifth	ju've nile	min i a ture'
drought	lic'o rice	leg er de main'
nook	a pos'tle	char i ot eer'
poor	ar'gen tine	an i mad vert'
roil	Ar min'ian	av oir du pois'
sauce	de co'rous	Cy clo pe'an
rhythm	cyc'la men	Eu ro pe'an
schism	so'journ er	spo li a'tion
root	cov'et ous	in'ter est ed

Lesson 197.

Words frequently mispronounced, or improperly accented.

pom'mel	ab'ject ness	nu mis'ma tist
bel'lows	ab'a cus	ig nit'i ble
fig'ure	ad'verse ly	Jan'u a ry
di rect'	Bur'gun dy	Feb'ru a ry
as'sets	Bed'ou in	in'ven to ry
je june'	en vi'rons	cor'ol la ry
ver'min	ex'ple tive	vi'o la ble
ran'sack	um'pi rage	rep'a ra ble
short'-lived	o'a sis	des'pi ca ble
so'journ	ar'se nic	bap'tis ter y
cais'son	ar'ti san	pres'by ter y

Lesson 198.

Words frequently mispronounced, or improperly accented.

ĭn'nāt̸e   e̸ẖŏl'er ie   sē'ere to ry
tēr'mĭt̸es   ḡŏn'fa lŏn   dĕe're to ry
wā̸y'lā̸y   çĕn'tu pl̸e   ĕx'ple to ry
slạ̈ug̸h'ter   rē'tro çēd̸e   eon sĭs'to ry
frăg̸'ĭl̸e   nū'ele ŭs   pre çĕp'to ry
eăr'rĭ̸ag̸e   çĕn'tau̸ ry   rĕp'er to ry
thȯr'ōu̸g̸h   eo qu̸ĕt'ry   eẖī rûr'g̣er y
se̸ẖĕd'ūl̸e   sto mă eẖ'ie   spērm a çē'tĭ
ḡrănd'̸eūr   ĭn'ter stĭç̸e   păn e ḡy̆r'ist
hir sūt̸e'   çe răm'ie   păn'e ḡy rīz̸e
bĕn'zĭn̸e   re vōlt'ing   mel lĭf'lu ̸eŭs

Lesson 199.

Words frequently mispronounced, or improperly accented.

ăḡ'ḡran dīz̸e   dĕm'on strāt̸e   tûr'mer ie
al'der man   tre mĕn'd̸oŭs   ɲ́ne mŏn'ie
Äl'eo răn   stu pĕn'd̸oŭs   vĭr'e lā̸y
ăl'g̣e brȧ   ḡŏv'ern ment   ĕx'pur ḡāt̸e
mĭş'ṱl̸e tō̸e   Är'a bie   ăm'ber-ḡrïs
prĕş'by ter   eŏm'bat ĭv̸e   mĭn'a ret
răşp'ber ry̆   eŏm'mu nĭst   ôr'de al
vĕn'ĭ şọn   eŏm'plaį şănç̸e   plăt'i nŭm
pŏş'i tĭv̸e   eŏn'vers̸e ly   fĕm'i nĭne
dĭş ẖŏn'est   dĭş ăş'ter   ḡĕn'ū ĭn̸e
çhĭv'al rie   drăm'a tĭst   por tĕnt'̸oŭs

Lesson 200.

Words to be carefully discriminated.

eôr'po ral, *an officer.*

eor pō're al, *bodily.*

dū'al ĭst, *a believer in two gods.*

dū'el ĭst, *one who fights a duel.*

de sçĕn'sion, *descent.*

dis sĕn'sion, *strife.*

çē're øŭs, *like wax.*

sē'ri øŭs, *grave; solemn.*

Sĭr'i ŭs, *the dog-star.*

vē'ni al, *pardonable.*

vē'nal, *mercenary; base.*

ăp'po ṣĭt¢, *suitable; fit.*

ŏp'po ṣĭt¢, *over against.*

ăe ela mā'tion, *a shout.*

ăe eli mā'tion, *inurement to a climate.*

ăn'a lȳz¢, *to separate.*

ăn'nal īz¢, *to record.*

ôr'a el¢, *a prophet.*

aŭ'ri el¢, *the external ear.*

Lesson 201.

The words opposite one another in the lines have nearly the same meaning, and are called *Synonyms*.

aŭ'thor īz¢

ap pâr'ent

ae eôrd'ant

de pōrt'ment

dĭ dăe'tie

fla ġĭ'tiøŭs

ad hēr'ent

ĭn'di ġenç¢

sy̆e'o phant

här'bin ġer

eom mĭs'sion

ŏb'vi øŭs

eŏn'so nant

de mēạn'or

pre çĕp'tĭv¢

a trō'ciøŭs

pär'ti ṣăn

pĕn'ū ry

pär'a sīt¢

pre eûr'sor

em pow'er

ĕv'i dent

a ġrēe'ing

be hāv'ior

in strŭet'ĭv¢

out rā'ġ¢øŭs

fŏl'lōw̶ er

pŏv'er ty

flăt'ter er

fōr¢ rŭn'ner

Lesson 202.

to̤, *towards; unto.*	vāne̸, *a weathercock.*
tōō, *also.*	vāi̸n, *proud; empty.*
two̤, *one and one.*	ve̤i̸n, *a blood-vessel.*
tre̤y̸, *three at cards.*	wāste̸, *to consume; loss.*
trāy̸, *a shallow vessel.*	wāi̸st, *part of the body.*
vāle̸, *a valley; a dell.*	wāre̸, *merchandise.*
ve̤i̸l, *a cover; a curtain.*	we̸ār, *to use; to waste.*
wāi̸t, *to tarry; to stay.*	wāy̸, *a road; manner.*
we̤i̸gh̸t, *heaviness; load.*	we̤i̸gh̸, *to balance.*
we̤i̸ghe̸d, *balanced.*	wēek, *seven days.*
wāde̸, *to walk in water.*	we̸ak, *not strong.*
wĕth'er, *a sheep.*	wŏŏd, *timber; a forest.*
we̸ăth'er, *state of the air.*	wo̤u̸ld, *preterit of will.*

Lesson 203.

Words sometimes incorrectly pronounced alike, but which should be carefully discriminated.

līne̸	loin	ᴄrēek	ᴇrĭck	sĕx	sĕets
lō̤am	lōōm	pīnt	point	yŏn	ya̤w̸n
los̤e̸	lōōse̸	săt	sŏt	lē̸ast	lĕst
môrn	mō̸urn	phās̤e̸	fāᴄe̸	sera̤w̸l	serōll
rout	ro̤ut̸e̸	la̤n̸d	lôrd	tĕnts	tĕnse̸
sta̤l̸k	stŏck	ē̸ast	ye̤ạst	wĭth	wĭthe̸
ᴄăn	kĕn	da̤w̸n	dŏn	ᴄlōs̤e̸	ᴄlōthe̸s̤
blánch	blĕnch	dōse̸	dōze̸	ᴄō̸ars̤e̸	ᴄôrse̸
wa̤nt	wŏnt	wĕn	whĕn	whīte̸	wĭgh̸t
wăx	whăcks	ä̤ms̤	ärms̤	mōōr	mōre̸

Lesson 204.

Words nearly alike in Sound, to be carefully distinguished.

as sāy'	es sāy'	ĕp'ie	ĕp'oeļ
de çēạse'	dis ēạṣẹ'	bēạ'eọn	bĕck'ọn
de sẹ́ent'	dis sĕnt'	eŏf'fin	eôụgh'ing
de vīçẹ́'	de vīṣẹ́'	ḡrĭsẹ́'ly	ḡrĭṣ'ly
hụz zä'	hụṣ ṣär'	dī'verṣ	dī'versẹ́
in tĕnsẹ́'	in tĕnts'	eļō'ral	eŏr'al
a loud'	al lowẹ́d'	ḡănt'let	ḡäụnt'let
im mẽrsẹ́'	a mẽrçẹ́'	mū'ṣie	mū'çie
af fēet'	ef fēet'	răd'ish	rĕd'dish
e lūdẹ́'	al lūdẹ́'	seūlp'tor	seūlpt'ūrẹ́
Ċäs'tīlẹ́	eàst'-stēel	hŭm'blẹ́	ŭm'bel

Lesson 205.

as çĕnt', *steepness.*
as sĕnt', *agreement.*
an̲'eļor, *for a ship.*
an̲k'er, *a liquid measure.*
ạl'ter, *to change.* [*fice.*
ạl'tar, *a place for sacri-*
au̲'ḡer, *an instrument.*
au̲'ḡur, *to foretell.*
bûr'rōẉ, *hole for shelter.*
bòr'ōụḡļ *a corporate town.*
bōld'er, *more bold.*
bōẉl'der, *a large pebble.*

bur'y (bĕr'rў), *to cover with earth.*
bĕr'ry, *a small fruit.*
eăn'non, *a great gun.*
eăn'on, *a rule or law.*
çēẏl'ing, *top of a room.*
sēạl'ing, *as with wax.*
çĕl'lar, *a lower room.*
sĕl'ler, *one who sells.*
çĕs'sion, *a giving up.*
sĕs'sion, *a sitting.*
eọ́ụṣ'ịn, *a relation.*
eòz'ẹ́n, *to cheat.*

Lesson 206.

çĕn'sū al, *of the census.*
sĕn'sū al, *carnal.*
ҽoun'çil, *an assembly.*
ҽoun'sel, *advice.* [*cloth.*
ҽăn'vas, *a kind of coarse*
ҽăn'vass, *to discuss.*
ҽrew'el, *worsted yarn.*
ҽru̯'el, *inhuman; savage.*
çy̆g̃'net, *a young swan.*
sĭg̃'net, *a seal.*
ҽẖŏl'er, *anger; wrath.*
ҽŏl'lar, *for the neck.*
fĭl'ter, *to strain.*

phĭl'ter, *a love-charm.*
g̃rҿāt'er, *larger.*
g̃rā'ter, *that which grates.*
hō'ly, *sacred; pure.*
ẉhōl'ly, *entirely.*
mär'tin, *a bird.*   [*sel.*
mär'ten, *a kind of wea-*
măn'ner, *form; method.*
măn'or, *district.* [*place.*
măn'tҽl, *shelf over a fire-*
măn'tlҽ, *a cloak.*
mär'tial, *warlike.*
mär'shal, *an officer.*

Lesson 207.

Words nearly alike in Sound, to be carefully distinguished.

ҽŏn'so nançҿ	ҽŏn'so nants	çĕn'sus	sĕn'seş
e ly̆ş'i an	e lĭş'ion	Lăt'in	lăt'ten
e mēr'sion	im mēr'sion	ҽŏn'çert	ҽŏn'sôrt
fôr'mer ly	fôrm'al ly	ҽôr'nĭçҿ	Ҽôrn'ish
pàss'a blҿ	păs'si blҿ	hăl'lōẉ	hā'lō
pe tĭ'tion	par tĭ'tion	rĕl'ie	rĕl'iet
ҽŏm'i ty	ҽom mĭt'tee	ôr'der	ôrd'ūrҿ
dĕp ra vā'tion	dĕp ri vā'tion	fä'ther	fär'ther
ve răç'i ty	vo răç'i ty	plȧi̯nt'iff	plȧi̯nt'īvҿ
stā'tion a ry	stā'tion er y	pā'tiençҿ	pā'tients

Lesson 208.

Words nearly alike in Sound, to be carefully distinguished.

bīl¢	boil	ad hēr'enç¢	ad hēr'ents
wĭḡ	whĭḡ	ꞓŏn fi dănt'	ꞓŏn'fi dent
Gŏd	ḡaᵤd	at tĕnd'anç¢	at tĕnd'ants
dånç¢	däᵤnts	ăe'çi denç¢	ăe'çi dents
dōm¢	dōōm	e lĭç'it	il lĭç'it
whēel	wēₐl	ĕm'i nenç¢	ĭm'mi nenç¢
lēₐs¢	lēeṣ	e rŭp'tion	ir rŭp'tion
sĕns¢	sĭnç¢	săl'a ry	çĕl'er y
drŏss	draᵥs̱	băr'ren ness	băr'on ess
whĭt	wĭt	prŏph'e çy̆	prŏph'e sȳ

Lesson 209.

mĕd'al, *a stamped coin.*	pĕn'çil, *used for writing.*
mĕd'dl¢, *to interfere.*	pĕn'sĭl¢, *hanging.*
mī'nor, *one under age.*	pĕt'ty, *small; little.*
mī'ner, *a worker in mines.*	pĕt'ĭʈ, *a term in law.*
mīt'y, *full of mites.*	pŏm'aç¢, *ground apples.*
mĭgʜt'y, *powerful.*	pŭm'ːç¢, *a spongy stone.*
nā'val, *of ships.*	rĭḡ'or, *severity; stiffness.*
nā'v¢l, *the central part.*	rĭḡ'ḡer, *one who rigs.*
çĕn'sor, *one who censures.*	sŭck'er, *a kind of fish.*
çĕns'er, *a pan for incense.*	sŭe'ꞓor, *help; assistance.*
păn'nel, *a kind of saddle.*	sûr'plus, *excess.*
păn'el, *a jury roll.*	sûr'plĭç¢, *a clerical dress.*

Lesson 210.

păl′let, *a small bed.*	eŏm′pli ment, *regard.*
păl′atɇ, *part of the mouth.*	eŏm′ple ment, *fullness.*
păl′ettɇ, *an oval board.*	eoun′sel or, *an adviser.*
ĕm′i ḡrātɇ, *to move out.*	eoun′çil or, *member of a*
ĭm′mi ḡrātɇ, *to move in.*	*council.* [*straight.*
eăs′tor, *the beaver.*	strāi̵ḡht′ɇn, *to make*
eȧst′er, *one who casts.*	strāi̵t′ɇn, *to narrow.*
eûr′rent, *running.*	eăl′en dar, *an almanac.*
cûr′rant, *a small fruit.*	eăl′en der, *a hot press.*
eăp′i tol, *a public edifice.*	sŭt′ler, *an army trader.*
eăp′i tal, *principal.*	sŭɓ′tler, *more subtle.*

Lesson 211.

Words which require Care in Spelling.

jĭlt	dŏl′lar	rĭp′plɇ	năt′ū ral
ġȳrɇ	seɓŏl′ar	trĭp′lɇ	ḡŭt′tur al
jōẘl	ḡrăp′plɇ	pŏp′py	lĭt′er al
trŏll	chăp′el	eŏp′y	dĭz′zi ly
ḡōᶏl	rĕn′net	sŭn′ny	bus̲′i ly
ḵnŏll	sĕn′atɇ	mȯn′ɇy	vĕr′ti eal
dōlɇ	frĕck′lɇ	ḡlĭm′mer	är′ti elɇ
tûrf	shĕk′ɇl	prĭm′er	dū′te ɵŭs
vĕrb	wĭt′ty	trĕᶏd′lɇ	bɇᶏū′te ɵŭs
pīrn	çĭt′y	pĕd′dlɇ	fĭn′i eal
pĕrk	hŏp′per	eŏd′dlɇ	pĭn′na elɇ
sûrd	prŏp′er	mŏd′el	çȳn′ie al

Lesson 212.

Words which require Care in Spelling.

scrĕam	cŏm'et	pĕb'ble	ĭn ter çēde'
scrēen	vŏm'it	rĕb'el	sū per sēde'
shĕave	plŭm'met	sĭb'yl	cŏl'o nize
shēet	sŭm'mit	spĭn'et	ăd ver tīse'
shĭeld	vĕr'y	lĭn'net	păr'a lȳze
twīrl	mĕr'ry	căm'el	sē'cre çy
chûrl	bŏd'y	trăm'mel	ĕc'sta sy
clērk	shŏd'dy	măm'mal	văç'il late
quĭrk	mŭd'dy	sĕv'en	făs'çi nate
fraud	stŭd'y	hĕav'en	cō ēr'cion
brŏad	gŭin'ea	păr'rot	de tēr'sion
awĕd	nĭn'ny	clăr'et	ex ēr'tion

Lesson 213.

Words which require Care in Spelling.

grĭef	do'ing	a bўss'	hĭd'e ous
shĕaf	stew'ing	a mĭss'	prē'vi ous
gŭile	yeo'man	as sĕss'	ĭm'pi ous
exĭle	chlō'ral	ăb'sçess	ā'que ous
rĕnd	know'ing	sĭck'le	păr'ti cle
wrĕnch	gō'ing	nĭck'el	crĭt'i cal
dĕarth	con dōle'	tăl'ents	dĭl'i gent
wŏrth	con trōl'	băl'ançe	ĕl'e gant
mīrth	en rōll'	sī'lençe	făl'li ble
ĕarth	dis pĕl'	com pēer'	prĕl'a çy
spûrt	fōre tĕll'	ad hēre'	jĕal'ous y

Lesson 214.

Words which require Care in Spelling.

whĭch	stŏm'aeḥ	re prĭēvĕ'	in ĭ'tial
dĭṭch	saụ'sagĕ	eon çĕịvĕ'	of fĭ'cial
fĕūd	wõrd'y	de grād̄ĕ'	es sĕn'tial
sū̧d	tûr'gid	a frāịd'	sol stĭ'tial
pruḍĕ	vẽr'ger	pre pârĕ'	a bŭn'dant
wōōĕd	vīr'tuĕ	for bĕâr'	de pĕnd'ent
baḷk	lĕø̧p'ard	bär'ter	in vẹịgḥ'er
shaẉl	lĕp'er	tär'tar	be trāy'er
ḡuịṣĕ	făm'ịnĕ	mär'tyr	dī'a lŏḡu̧ĕ
sīgḥs	ḡăm'mon	sue çēed'	dȳ năm'ies
flịĕṣ	săḷm'ċn	ae çēdĕ'	me eḥăn'ies

Lesson 215.

Words which require Care in Spelling.

wịeld	seăn'dal	se rēnę'	ăn'no tātę
wẹịrd	hăn'dlę	un ₵lēạn'	ăn'o dȳnę
swālę	₵lăm'or	be twēen'	eŏl on nādę'
swāịn	ḡrăm'mar	ma rïnę'	sĕr e nādę'
stôrm	hăm'mer	₵om plētę'	dŏm i nēer'
swạrm	päḷm'er	de fēạt'	bĕl ve dērę'
sçȳthę	sā'tyr	de çēịt'	pĕn'ni less
ẉrīthę	trāị'tor	₵ō ērçę'	mȯn'ęy less
sịęvę	wāịt'er	dis bûrsę'	jǒe'ū lar
ḡïvę	₵rā'ter	dis pērsę'	jŏck'ęy ing

Lesson 216.

Words which require Care in Spelling.

skẹịn	văl'id	kīr'tlę	pŏl'i çy
slāịn	săl'ad	tûr'tlę	lĕḡ'a çy
₵rānę	măl'let	fēr'tilę	₵ûr'ti laḡę
sẉōrd	văl'et	myr'tlę	sȳn'a ḡōḡụę
bōạst	brēez'y	wĭd'ḡęon	₵ŏd'i çil
ḡḥ̇ōst	ḡrēạṣ'y	pĭḡ'ęon	dŏm'i çilę
quéer	ḡär'dęn	măl'ïçę	vēr'sa tĭlę
brịęf	pär'dȯn	păl'açę	hȳp'o ₵rītę
spōkę	ē'vịl	tôr'tǫịsę	hĭp'po drōmę
₵rōạk	ēạ'ḡlę	môr'tĭsę	sǫēn'er y
sĕlf	pōlę'ăx	sĕl'vaḡę	plē'na ry
sȳlph	pōụlt'ry	pŏr'riḏ̇ḡę	dēạn'er y

Lesson 217.

Words which require Care in Spelling.

zine	eŏl'leġe	eon fẽr'	ū tĕn'sil
brĭnk	ḳnŏẁl'eḋġe	a stīr'	pre hĕn'sīle
fôṵġht	lĕẚth'er	oe eûr'	fa tĭġṵ'ing
eaṵġht	tĕth'er	ef fāçe	be lēẚ'ġṵer
ẁrôṵġht	eaṵ'eus	e rāse	sĭ lĭ'ceøŭs
fūṣe	maẁk'ish	chas tĭṣe'	vex ā'tiøŭs
newṣ	aṵ'thor	bap tīze'	fa çē'tiøŭs
vïewṣ	aẁn'ing	a chïeve	sus pī'cion
chōōṣe	ăr'id	per çeïve	po ṣi'tion
wōōęṣ	ḥeïr'shĭp	be rēẚve	in çĭṣ'ion
ōōze	âïr'y	re nown'	de rĭṣ'ion
ẁhoṣe	eăr'ry	re nounçe	e dĭ'tion

Lesson 218.

Words which require Care in Spelling.

ẽẚrl	răṉ'eȯr	in vāde	dī ûr'nal
ḳnûrl	eăṉ'ker	up brāïd'	hī bẽr'nal
shĭrk	flŭx'ion	ur bāne	at tõr'nęy
jẽrk	sṵe'tion	or dāïn'	de tẽr'ġent
pĭth	hŏs'pïçe	a dïeu'	eon tā'ġïŏn
mȳth	aṵ'spïçe	im brṵe	her bā'ceøŭs
ḡrōẁth	bŏt'tom	pre çēde	frŏl'ie sȯme
lōẚth	aṵ'tumṉ	pro çeed'	frŏl'ick ing
lōẚthe	trŭnn'ion	re dēem'	de prĕs'sion
elōthe	bŭn'ion	ex trēme	dis erĕ'tion

Lesson 219.

Words which require Care in Spelling.

rĭsk	coŭp'le	wry'ness	vē'hĭ cle
wrĭst	cŭp'board	rī'ot	tўp'ic al
shrĕd	cho'rus	lў'rist	ŏb'sta cle
drĕad	pō'rŏus	li'vre	prō'to col
scheme	hĭll'y	tĕn'on	mўs'tic al
chĭef	lĭl'y	pĕn'non	mĭs'ti ness
sĭege	sēat	săn'dal	rŏs'trum	rĕe're ant
sēat	căn'dle	phăn'tom	rĕck'ŏn er
sēethe	nū'tant	făn'ion	wrĕtch'ed ly
kēyed	neū'ter	vĕr'sion	ŏf'fi çer
twēed	nūi'sançe	tĕr'tian	ŏph'ĭ cleide

Lesson 220.

Words containing silent Letters.

thôught	hănd'some	re doubt'	hĕe'a tomb
wrēathe	vĭct'uals	re scĭnd'	scī'o lĭst
wrēath	scĭs'sors	gneĭs'sose	cō a lĕsçe'
rhŏmb	schŏt'tĭsh	be nĭgn'	ăp'o thĕgm
gnăt	gnō'mon	cam pāĭgn'	dī'a phrăgm
rōgue	fŏr'eĭgn	ar rāĭgn'	psȳ'chĭc al
gnaw	dough'ty	op pūgn'	săc'cha rīne
gnăsh	haught'y	re sĭgn'	rheu măt'ĭc
gnärl	chrŏn'ĭc	de lĭght'	rhăp'so dy
gnōme	daugh'ter	ex pūgn'	rhĕt'o rĭc
phlĕgm	ghăst'ly	af frīght'	ca tärrh'al

Sp. 9.

Lesson 221.

Silent Letters.

tauǥht	hon'est	ea tärrh'	pneu măt'ics
source	gher'kin	eon děmn'	psal'ter ў
brouǥht	chalk'y	de měssn'	pneu mō'ni å
realm	is'l'and	de pōt'	rhī nŏç'e rŏs
vault	năph'thå	bûrgh'er	rĕn'dez vous
knŏb	grĭs'tle	ealk'er	jĕop'ard ў
quälm	thrŏs'tle	rhŏm'boid	hĕm'or rhage
wrŏth	chris'ten	mē'sis	rhīz'o pŏd
frauǥht	jĕop'ard	ptĭş'an	ptär'mi ǥan
knŏck	wrĭg'ǥle	psў'ehie	pseū'do nўm
knīfe	brĭs'tle	rhўm'er	psälm'ist rў

Lesson 222.

Words liable to be misspelled.

trĕs'tle	ǥlū'ey ness	eol lĕet'i ble
pa paw'	erўs'tal līne	e räs'a ble
ǥey'ser	ehrўs'a lĭs	ae eôr'dĭ on
ǥauǥ'ing	läeh'ry mōse	săç er dō'tal
eo lōǥne'	kĕr'o sēne	ĕf fer vĕs'çençe
qua drĭlle'	ǥlўç'er ĭnǥ	tran quĭl'li ty
skў'ey	är'ǥo naut	eom mĭt'ti ble
sôr'ǥhum	fôre bōd'ing	eôr us eā'tion
sur vey'	ex chĕq'uer	măe a rō'nĭ
stärve'ling	sĭb'yl līne	pĭe'ea lĭl lĭ
prō'ǥrämme	sĭb'i lant	fĭl'i bŭs ter

Lesson 223.

Words liable to be misspelled.

flĕạm	ǵȳ'ing	ġĕn e ăl'o ġy
ḡlўph	wēe'v/l	băɛ ɛa lạ/'re atǿ
lïēġǿ	lăɛ'ɋ/er	ăb o rĭġ'i nēṣ
ɛuïsh́	du ĕt'	är ɛh́æ ŏl'o ġy
tä/nt	quạr tĕt'	ăs a fĕt'i dà
dräṕ	phē'nix	ĕr y sĭp'e las
flęçhǿ	rōḡ/'ish	hō mo ġē'ne ǿŭs
frêrǿ	whęy'ǿў	hў per ɛrĭt'i çĭṣm
järdǿṣ	lĕḏġ'er	ịɛh́ thy ŏl'o ġy
ɛrўpt	săch'el	ĭḡ'nis-făt ū ŭs
soạ/	lăr'yṉx	lăck a dä/'ṣi ɛal

Lesson 224.

Words frequently mispronounced.

fôr'tress	dăn'druff	prŏd'ūçǿ	ɛon çĭsǿ'
ɛär'bīnǿ	frăn'chĭṣǿ	ɛŏm'bat	dĭṣ ōẃn'
ɛh́lō'rĭdǿ	hŏm'aġǿ	thĭth'er	dĭṣ dä/n'
ɛŏf'fee	rh́ụ'bärb	ō'nyx	dĭ vŭlġǿ'
ɛŏm'radǿ	ɛŏv'ert	dĭṣ ärm'	ex tŏl'
saạ/'çer	mā'tron	jo ɛōsǿ'	for bădǿ'
dĕɛ'adǿ	mŏn'ad	bǿûr ġǿois'	suf fūṣǿ'
quĭn'ṣў	pā'tron	Ɛäy ĕnnǿ'	pos sĕss'
ḡăl'lòẃs	lĭth'arġǿ	ɛon toạ/r'	fârǿ wĕll'
mĭṣ'lǿ	pär'trĭḏġǿ	dĭ vêrġǿ'	be nēạth'
faạ/'çet	wạ'ter	dĭ vêrt'	re sōạ/rçǿ'

Lesson 225.

Words frequently mispronounced.

dī'a mȯnd	păr'a dīsḙ	çin choͫ'nȧ
chăn de lĩer'	ā'li as	in vĕĩ'ğlḙ
ğrăn'a ry	păr'a chṳtḙ	stra tē'ği e
coṳ'rĭ er	pōt-poṳr ri'	ex cûr'sion
ēğ'lan tĩnḙ	hȳ'ği ēnḙ	a cous'ti es
sôr'çer y	cŏn'fis cātḙ	an chō'vy
ĕx'tir pātḙ	psăl'mo dȳ	pa lä'ver
côr'di al	ğṳärd'ĭ an	Caṳ cā'sian
côr'ri dôr	cŏm'mu nĭsm	ap păr'el
ğăs̩'e ọus	sub al'tern	so prä'no
dŏç'i blḙ	coụ rā'ğḙọus	ĭm mor tĕllḙ'

Lesson 226.

Words liable to be misspelled.

sȯm'er saṳlt	how'itz er	băr'y tōnḙ
stĭm'ū lŭs	sȳc'a mōrḙ	bĭl'lings ğātḙ
sĭl'houͫ ĕttḙ	a brĭḋğ'ment	brȳ'o ny
pa vĭl'ion	ăd'di blḙ	çĕn'ti ped
quin tĭll'ion	æs thĕt'ie	çĭm'e ter
çĭ vĭl'ian	ăl'che my	col'an der
çĕn'ti ğrăm	är'que bŭsḙ	cop'i er
ma nĭl'lȧ	āṷ lăn'tus	nas tûr'tium
ḙū'pho nȳ	as bĕs'tus	chĭe'o ry
prŏs'e lȳtḙ	as çĕnd'ant	heĩ'nọus ness
pū'tre fȳ	sȳz'y ğy	dĕb o nâĩr'
pro bŏs'çis	bär'be cūḙ	pôr'phy ry

Lesson 227.

Words liable to be misspelled.

bạl'driė   mal fēạ'ṣançę   ėal lĭḡ'ra phy
bän'yan   sûr'çin̄ ḡlę   dўs'en tĕr y
bạ𝈵'blę   plęū'ri sy   rĕm i nĭs'çençę
la pĕl'   pôr'çe lain   hў pŏė'ri sy
kẽr'chĭęf   ŏs'çil lātę   hȳ pŏt'e nūsę
ġnŏs'tiė   dĕl'e blę   syn ēė'do ė𝈵e
bŭt'-ĕnd   lạ𝈵'da nŭm   sī dē're al
ėăm'phēnę   ėrўs'tal līzę   ăd sęi tĭ'tiŏŭs
ėă𝈵ch'up   pŏl'y ḡlŏt   ăm ạ𝈵 rō'sis
çĕss'-pōōl   ḡ𝈵er rĭl'là   lĭll i pū'tian
çi ḡär'   quin tĕs'sençę   lĭl i ā'ceęŭs

Lesson 228.

Words liable to be misspelled.

ėlew   ėoif'fūrę   ėon fēė'tion ĕr y
ėlĭnch   flĕ𝈵ġę'ling   klĕp to mā'ni à
slęūth   ă𝈵'ḡ𝈵an   ėôr nu ėō'pi à
blŏndę   çhe nĭllę'   ėŏt y lĕd'o nęŭs
ḡlēbę   çhe mïṣę'   dī ū tûr'ni ty
ġȳvęṣ   çhăs'sęûr   tẽrp sie𝈵 o rē'an
ḡ𝈵ȳ   çhĕv'ron   me tĕmp sy ė𝈵ō'sis
ėrŭ𝈵ch   ėôr'ymb   mē te ŏr'o lītę
tęŭch   e lẹvę'   pĕr ip nęū'mo ny
kräạl   hŏḡṣ'hėạd   phär ma ėo pœ'ià
chïntz   mēer'sçhạ𝈵m   phär ma çęū'tiė al
çïerġę   bû𝈵r'-stōnę   săė ė𝈵a rĭf'er ęŭs

Lesson 229.

Words liable to be misspelled or mispronounced.

ĕl e phan tī′a sis

păr a di sī′ae al

păr a pher nā′li ȧ

vĕr i si mĭl′i tūdę

tĭn tin năb ū lā′tion

sū per e rŏḡ′a tĭvę

pū sil la nĭm′i ty

phan tăṣ ma ḡō′ri ȧ

ŏb′li ḡa tō ri ly

ĭd i o sўn′era sy

ĭr re mē′di a blę

ĭp e eae ū ăn′hȧ

ĭr re eŏḡ′ni za blę

ḡū ber na tō′ri al

ĕl ee mŏs′y na ry

pŏl y eot y lē′don

hĕt er o ḡē′ne ǿŭs

hī e ro ḡlўph′ie al

hўp o eḫon drī′ae al

his tō ri ŏḡ′ra pher

in dĭs′so lu blę ness

in dĭs′pu ta blę ness

ĕr y si pĕl′a tǿŭs

ĭr rĕf′ra ḡa blę ness

Lesson 230.

Words of irregular Pronunciation.

ŏf (ŏv)	tǿŭgh (tŭf)	trôǿgh (trawf)
sīcę (sīz)	hǿŭgh (hŏk)	buṣ′ў (bĭz′ў)
tïgę (tēj)	fiôrd (fyôrd)	ma′nў (mĕn′ў)
sayṣ (sĕz)	buoў (bwoў)	pret′tў (prĭt′tў)
said (sĕd)	eôǿgh (kawf)	wom′en (wĭm′en)
loir (lwär)	monⱦ (mōng)	eañ ȯn′ (kan yŭn′)
a′nў (ĕn′ў)	roǿgę (rōōzh)	sä lōn̲′ (sä lōng′)
newt (nūt)	mauvę (mōv)	çhăp′eau (shăp′o)
beaux (bōz)	ruçhę (rōōsh)	çha teau′ (sha tō′)
onçę (wŭns)	Czĕeḫ (tchĕk)	ero qǿeⱦ′ (kro kā′)
ī′rǿn (ī′urn)	eăf′é (kăf′ä)	men ägę′ (-äzh′)

Lesson 231.

Words of irregular Pronunciation.

pa tois' (pat wạ')
bï joụ' (be zhōō')
p̷a̷t̷h̷ïṣ'i⦵ (tĭz'ik)
bū'reau (bū'ro)
E̱n'g̅lish (ĭng'g̅lish)
flăm'beau (flăm'bo)
hauţ'boy (hō'boy)
hï⦵'⦵ø̷ŭgh (hĭk'kup)
rīg̷h̷t'eoŭs (rī'chus)
çhăm'ø̷ïṣ̷ (shăm'mў)
boụ'doir (bōō'dwôr)
ser'g̅eạnt (sär'jent)

boụ q̷u̷e̷ţ' (bōō kā')
breech'eṣ (brĭch'ez)
pôr'pọïṣ̷ (pôr'pus)
a g̅ain' (a g̅ĕn')
diṣ cẽrn' (diz zẽrn')
e nø̷ŭgh' (e nŭf')
e̱n nuï' (ŏng nwē')
ron deau' (ron dō')
vig̷ñ ĕttø̷' (vin yĕt')
squir'rel (*or* skwŭr'rel)
suf fīçø̷' (suf fīz')
⦵ôr'teg̷ø̷ (kôr'tāzh)

Lesson 232.

Words of irregular Pronunciation.

sø̷ŭgh (sŭf)
myrrḥ (mẽr)
suăvø̷ (swāv)
shew (shō)
strew (strụ)
boụffø̷ (bōōf)
nōm (nōng)
⦵lø̷ŭgh (klŭf)
née (nā)
g̅ḥat (g̅awt)
⦵rø̷ûx̷ (krû)

men ăg'e rï̷ø̷ (men ăzh'e rў)
ci ce rō'ne (chē che- *or* sĭs'e-)
çhĕv'aux-de-frïṣø̷ (shĕv'o de frēz)
păp'ier-mä çhe̱ (păp'yā mä shā)
dé ⦵ŏl le té' (dā kol le tā')
tïe-doụ loụ rø̷ụx̷' (tĭk dōō lōō rōō')
vẽr mï cĕl'lï (-chĕl'lï *or* -sĕl'lï)
sū per fï'ciȩṣ (sū per fĭsh'ēz)
ră tion ā'le (răsh un ā'le)
ḥä bĭt ụ é (ä bĭt ụ ā')
hăl le lū'jàḥ (hăl le lū'yȧ)

Lesson 233.

Words of irregular Pronunciation.

buş′ı̈ ness (bĭz′nes) rŏq′ụe laurę́ (rŏk′e lōr)

eolo nel (kûr′nel) săe′ri fīcę́ (săk′rĭ fīz)

hau tęûr′ (hō tûr′) çhęf-d′œuvrę́ (shā dōōvr′)

ƀdĕll′ium (dĕl′yum) ĕs eri toirę́ (ĕs krĭ twôr′)

euï răss′ (kwe răs′) bellę́ş-lĕt′tręş (bel lĕt′ter)

ḡauçhę́ rı̈ē′ (ḡōsh rē′) mĭ́ḡñ on ettę́ (mĭn yon ĕt′)

trọụş seau′ (trōō sō′) fụęḥ′si ȧ (fōōk′sĭ ȧ)

ḡŭn′ẇalę́ (ḡŭn′nel) re vęı̈′l′lę (re vāl′yā)

däḥ′lia (däl′yȧ) păp ę tę́rı̈ē′ (păp a trē′)

soi ręe′ (swä rä′) sur vęı̈′l′lançę́ (-vāl′yans)

săp′phīrę́ (săf′ı̈r) Plĕ′ia dęş (plĕ′ya dēz)

eōḡ″ñae (kōn′yak)

Lesson 234.

Words of irregular Pronunciation.

nĕs′ciençę́ (nĕsh′ens) re çhêr çhé′ (rŭh shêr shā′)

ba ręgę́ (ba räzh′) sō brī qụ̈ęt′ (sō bre kā′)

dĭph′thong (dĭf′-) āı̈d′-de-eamp (ād′de kŏng)

sōl′dier (sōl′jer) mag ġı̈ō′re (mad jō′ra)

fôrt′ūnę́ (fôrt′yụn) mădę́ moi şĕllę́ (-mwạ zĕl′)

nĕph′ew (nĕf′yụ) flę́ụr-de-lı̈ş′ (flụr de lē′)

lĕt′tuçę́ (lĕt′tis) dĕb au çhēe′ (dĕb o shē′)

en trée′ (ŏng trä′) rĕş er vôı̈r′ (rĕz er vwôr′)

rę gĭmę́ (rā zhĕm′) ƀı̈s tĕdd′fŏd (īs tĕth′fŏd)

seru toirę́ (skru twôr′) prō té gé′ (prō tā zhā′)

phy şïqụ̈ę́ (fē zēk′) de nọụę́men̈ẗ (-nōō′mong)

Lesson 235.

Words of irregular Pronunciation.

erĭ tïqu̶é' (krĭ tēk') en̶ e̶ōr̶é' (ŏng kōr')

pen̶ çhan̶ṯ' (pŏng shŏng') sé an̶ç̶é' (sā ŏngs')

çhïg̶'ñon̶ (shēn'yŏng) mor çeau' (mor sō')

çha le̶ṯ' (sha lā') dan̶ s̶e̶ûs̶é' (dŏng zûrz')

é l̶an̶' (ā lăng') sang-froid' (sŏng frwä')

mĕm'oir (mĕm'wor) qu̶ï vïv̶é (kē vēv)

mon̶ s̶ï̶e̶u̶r' (mo sēr') fau̶x päs̶' (fō pä')

blanc-man̶g̶é' (blo-mŏnj') bŏn̶ tŏn̶ (bŏng tŏng)

a men̶d̶é' (a mŏngd') bŏn̶'mō̶t̶ (bŏng'mō)

çen tïm̶é' (sŏn tēm') mil lie̶ṯ' (mi lyā')

bĭv'øuăe (bĭv'wăk) sä van̶ṯ' (sä vŏng')

Lesson 236.

Names of Men.

Chärlẹṣ	Ăd'am	Hăr'old	Ā'så
Frănk	Ăl'bert	Hĕn'ry	Băṣ'il
Gẹôrgẹ	Ăn'drew	Hō'mer	Ċā'leb
Hūgh	Är'thur	Ī'ṣaảe	Çē'phas
Jāmẹṣ	Ċlăr'ençẹ	Jā'eob	Çȳ'rus
Jōb	Dā'vid	Jō'ṣeph	Ēu'ġēnẹ
Jŏhn	Ĕd'ward	Lew'is	Fē'lix
Lūkẹ	Ĕd'win	Nō'åh	Jā'bez
Märk	Ĕz'rå	Păt'rick	Lĕọn'ard
Saṵl	Frăn'çis	Pē'ter	Mō'ṣeṣ
Rălph	Ḡĭl'bert	Wĭll'iam	Rŏb'ert

Lesson 237.

Names of Men.

Hĕr'bert	Ăb'sa lŏm	Ăl ex ăn'der
Hī'ram	Ăn'thŏ ny	Ăn dro nī'eus
Hŏr'açẹ	Bĕn'ja mĭn	Bar thŏl'o mew
Jā'sọn	E lī'jȧh	Eb en ē'zer
Jĕs'se	Fĕr'di nand	Em măn'ū el
Laẉ'rençẹ	Frĕd'er ick	E zē'ki el
Lē'vī	I ṣā'iȧh (-yȧ)	Jĕr e mī'ȧh
Lū'ther	Le ăn'der	Le ŏn'i das
Ŏs'ear	Ŏl'i ver	Na pō'le on
Phĭl'ip	Săm'ū el	The ŏph'i lŭs
Rĭch'ard	Tĭm'o thy̆	Zĕeh a rī'ȧh

Lesson 238.

Names of Women.

Ănnͤ	Ā′dȧ	Ĕs′thͤer	Lō′is
Blȧnchͤ	Ăg′nĕs̤	Ĕu′nĭçͤ	Lū′çy
Ēvͤ	Ăl′ĭçͤ	Ē′vȧ	Mā′bel
Ḡrāçͤ	Ăn′nȧ	Făn′ny	Mär′thȧ
Jānͤ	Bĕr′thȧ	Flō′rȧ	Mā′ry
Jēͤn	Ͼlăr′ȧ	Frän′çes	Mȳ′rȧ
Kātͤ	Ͼō′rȧ	Ḡĕr′trṳdͤ	Năn′çy
Maͤd	Ē′dith	Hĕl′en	Rā′chel
Māy	Ĕd′nȧ	Hăn′nȧh	Rͪō′dȧ
Pēͤrl	Ĕl′lȧ	Ī′dȧ	Sā′rȧh
Rṳth	Ĕm′mȧ	Laͤ′rȧ	Sū′s̤an

Lesson 239.

Names of Women.

Ā′my	Ăd′e līnͤ	A mē′li ȧ
Bĕt′sͤy	A măn′dȧ	Ăr a bĕl′lȧ
Brĭdͬ′ĝet	Bär′ba rȧ	Dͦr o thē′ȧ
Ͼhär′lottͤ	Bē′a trĭçͤ	E lĭz′a bĕth
Ͼͪlō′e	Dĕb′o rȧh	E văn′ĝe līnͤ
Dͦr′ͤas	E lī′zȧ	Fe lĭç′i ȧ
Dī′nȧh	Ĕm′i ly	Frĕd er ĭ′ͤȧ
Ĕl′len	Mär′ĝa ret	Ġͤôr ġi ăn′ȧ
Flͦr′ençͤ	Pris çĭl′lȧ	Ĭş a bĕl′lȧ
Ja nĕt′	Re bĕͤ′ͤȧ	La vĭn′i ȧ
Rͦ′s̤ȧ	Su s̤ăn′nȧ	Viͤ tō′ri ȧ

Lesson 240.

Abbreviations used in Writing and Printing.

A. or *Ans.*, Answer.
A. B., Bachelor of Arts.
A. C., or *B. C.*, Before Christ. [our Lord.
A. D., In the year of
A. M., Master of Arts; Before noon; In the year of the world.
Bart., Baronet.
Bbl., Barrel; barrels.
B. L., Bachelor of Laws.

Bro., Brother.
C. H., Court-House.
Co., Company; County.
C. O. D., Collect on delivery.
Cr., Credit. [ity.
D. D., Doctor of Divin-
Do., or *ditto*, The same.
Dr., Doctor; Debtor.
e. g. (exempli gratia), For example.

Lesson 241.

Abbreviations used in Writing and Printing.

Ed., Editor; Edition.
Eng., England; English.
Esq., Esquire. [forth.
Etc. (et cetera), And so
Fri., Friday.
Fahr., Fahrenheit.
F. R. S., Fellow of the Royal Society.
Gen., General; Genesis.
Gov., Governor.
G. P. O., General Post-Office.

H. B. M., Her Britannic Majesty.
Hhd., Hogshead.
H. R., House of Representatives.
Ibid., In the same place.
Id. (idem), The same.
i. e. (id est), That is.
Jas., James.
Jun. or *Jr.*, Junior.
Lat., Latitude.
Lb., Pound; pounds.

Lesson 242.

Abbreviations used in Writing and Printing.

LL. D., Doctor of Laws.
Long., Longitude.
L. S., Place of the Seal.
M., Monsieur.   [gress.
M. C., Member of Con-
Mon., Monday.   [cine.
M. D., Doctor of Medi-
Messrs., Gentlemen.
M. P., Member of Par-
liament.
Mr., Mister; Master.

Mrs., Mistress.
N., North.
N. A., North America.
MS., Manuscript.
No., Number.   [notice.
N. B. (nota bene), Take
pp., Pages.
Per., By the.   [ternoon.
P. M., Postmaster; Af-
P. O., Post-Office.
Prof., Professor.

Lesson 243.

Abbreviations used in Writing and Printing.

P. S., Postscript.
Pub. Doc., Public Doc-
ument.
Pxt., He painted it.
Sc., He engraved it.
Q. M., Quartermaster.
Rec'd., Received.
Rev., Reverend.
S., Shilling; South.
S. A., South America.
Sat., Saturday.
Sen., Senior; Senator.

St., Saint; Street.
Sun., Sunday.
Supt., Superintendent.
Thurs., Thursday.
Tues., Tuesday.
V., *vid.*, or *vide*, See.
Viz. (videlicet), Namely.
Vol., Volume.
Vs. (versus), Against.
Wed., Wednesday.
W. I., West Indies.
Wt., Weight.

Lesson 244.

Abbreviations of the States, with their Pronunciation.

Ala., Ăl a bȧ′mȧ.

Ark., Är′kan sa̤s̤.

Cal., Ꞓăl i fôr′nĭ ȧ.

Col. or *Colo.*, Ꞓŏl o rä′do.

Conn. or *Ct.*, Ꞓon nĕȼt′ĭ ȼut.

Del., Dĕl′a wârȼ.

Flor. or *Fla.*, Flŏr′ĭ dȧ.

Geo. or *Ga.*, Ġȼôr′ġĭ ȧ.

Ill., Ĭl lĭ nois̤′.

Ind., Ĭn dĭ ăn′ȧ.

Ia., Ī′o wȧ.

Kan., Kăn′sas.

Ky., Ken tŭck′y.

Lou. or *La.*, Lo̤ṳ ï s̤ï ȧ′nȧ.

Mass., Măs sa chū′setts.

Md., Mā′ry land.

Me., Māi̤nȼ.

Mich., Mĭçh′i ḡa̤n.

Minn., Mĭn ne sō′tȧ.

Miss., Mĭs sis sĭp′pĭ.

Mo., Mĭs so̤ṳ′rĭ.

Lesson 245.

Abbreviations of the States, with their Pronunciation.

Neb., Ne brăs′kȧ.

N. C., Nôrth Ꞓăr o lī′nȧ.

N. H., New Hămp′shirȼ.

N. J., New Jĕr′s̤ȼy̆.

Nev., Ne vä′dȧ.

N. Y., New Yôrk.

Or., Ŏr′e ḡon.

O., O hī′o.

Pa. or *Penn.*, Pĕnn sy̆l vā′nĭ ȧ.

R. I., Rㅐ̥ōdȼ Ī̤s̤l′and.

S. C., South Ꞓăr o lī′nȧ.

Tenn., Tĕn nes sēe′.

Tex., Tĕx′as.

Uh., Ū′täㅐ̥ (yōō′tä).

U. S. A., U nīt′ed Stătȼs̤ of A mĕr′i ȼȧ.

Va., Vīr ġĭn′ĭ ȧ.

Vt., Ver mŏnt′.

Wis., Wis ȼŏn′sin.

W. Va., Wĕst Vīr ġĭn′ĭ ȧ.

Lesson 246.

American and Foreign Geographical Names.

Ạl'ba nў	Bä'den	Ăl le g̶h̶e̶'ny
Ayr (âr)	Bạl'ti mōrꬲ	Ā'si à (ä'shĭ à)
Aulne (ōn)	Bor deaux' (-dō')	Çĭn çĭn nä'tĭ
Bŏs'ton	Çhĭ ĕạ'g̶o	Ḙ̄ŭ phrä'tēs̟
Çheẏ ĕnnꬲ'	-Çạ̄i'ro	Hä wạ̄i'ï
Mạ̄in	Cey'lŏn'	Păl'es tīnꬲ
Mo bĭlꬲ'	Ĭ's̟er (ē'zer)	Phĭl a dĕl'phĭ à
Pau (pō)	Mad rĭd'	Pў̆r'e nēes̟
Sạ̄ōnꬲ	Mil wạu̶'kee	S̶z̶ēg̶ ed ïn'
Sḙ̄inꬲ	Mon tä'nà	Vï ĕn'nà
T̶ham̶ꬲs̟ (tĕmz)	New Ôr'le ans̟	Wạsh'ing tȯn

Lesson 247.

Other Geographical Names of frequent Mispronunciation.

Guanaxuato (g̶wä nä hwä'to)	Aube (ōb)
Poughkeepsie (pō kĭp'sĭ)	Caen (kŏn̠)
Worcester (wŏŏs'ter)	Dieppe (dyĕp)
Youghiogheny (yŏh'ho g̶ä'nĭ)	Foix (fwä)
Newfoundland (nū'fund land)	Joux (zhōō)
Chuquisaca (chōō ke sä'kä̠)	Lisle (lēl)
Guatemala (g̶ạ te mä'là)	Moux (mōō)
Winnipiseogee (-pis sŏk'kĭ)	Oude (owd)
Venezuela (ven ĕ zwē'là)	Sioux (sōō)
Altamaha (ạl ta ma hạ')	Thau (tō)
Chautauqua (sha tạ'kwà)	Y (ī)

Lesson 248.

OF CHARACTERS USED IN PUNCTUATION.

A *Comma* [,] denotes the slightest degree of separation between the elements of a sentence.

A *Semicolon* [;] denotes a degree of separation somewhat greater than that indicated by a comma.

A *Colon* [:] marks a still greater degree of separation than a semicolon.

A *Period* [.] usually indicates the close of a sentence.

The *Interrogation Point* [?] is used at the end of a question.

The *Exclamation Point* [!] denotes astonishment or other emotion.

A *Hyphen* [-] is used to join words or syllables.

A *Dash* [—] marks a sudden break or stop in a sentence.

A *Parenthesis* [( )] includes words which might be left out without injuring the sense.

Brackets [ ] inclose words, etc., intended to explain or rectify what precedes or follows.

An *Apostrophe* ['] indicates the omission of one or more letters; or denotes the possessive case.

Quotation Marks [" "] show that the passage included, is taken from some other author.

OF CAPITAL LETTERS.

A *Capital* should begin: (1) the first word of every sentence, and of every line of poetry; (2) proper names of persons, places, months, and days; (3) all appellations of the Deity; (4) titles of honor; (5) names of things personified; (6) names denoting the race or nation of individuals; (7) adjectives derived from proper names; (8) the first word of a direct quotation or speech; (9) the principal words in the titles of books; (10) words denoting important events, the chief subject of a composition, etc. (11) The pronoun *I* and the interjection *O* are always capitals.